THE LITTLE BOOK OF POSITIVITY

A FIRST-AID KIT FOR YOUR WELL-BEING

FAYE EDWARDES

AND CO.

ALSO BY FAYE EDWARDES

BOOKS

The Science of Happiness in *From the Ashes: She is Ignited* (2022) with Louisa Herridge. Authors & Co.

and

A Life Less Ordinary in *Fearless Females* (2018) with Rebecca Lockwood.

PODCASTS

The Confidence, Happiness and Positivity Podcast

https://podcasts.apple.com/gb/podcast/the-confidence-happiness-and-positivity-podcast

and

The Sober Stories Podcast

https://podcasts.apple.com/gb/podcast/sober-stories-podcast

CONTENTS

DEDICATION

For Alfie and Honey, always.

ACKNOWLEDGEMENTS

This book is dedicated to my little people, Alfie and Honey, who are my inspiration, my motivation and who make me howl with laughter (and often sob huge, great tears) every single day. All this is for you and about you.

I won the friends lottery when it came to those crazy fools who chose to ride this journey called life with me: Kate Baldwin, Rebecca O'Donnell, Anne-Marie Watkinson, Stefanie Kaliszczak, Sarah McLachlan, Angela Gibson, Angie Procter, Kelly Steele, Becky Loto to name just a few of the absolute beauts in my life.

My parents, who are both hilarious and brilliant - for that I thank them.

To those who have been instrumental in my own personal growth: Niyc Pidgeon, Tina Pavlou, Debbie Walker, Lucinda Walton, Dani Wallace, Abigail Horne, Philippa Iles, Katie Cooper, Iona Russell, Melanie Deague and so many more incredible people who I am yet to come across.

To all the authors, writers and podcast hosts that have filled my head and my heart over the last few years. I learn something new every single day thanks to people being brave and vulnerable enough to share their stories, experiences, wisdom and learnings. Writing a book is like stripping a piece of your soul off and laying it out for the world to see. It's scary and chilly and raw and real. Those who write are truly putting themselves out there for the benefit of their readers and I realise that so much more now than ever before.

Always grateful,

Faye

WHAT IS THE POINT OF THIS BOOK?

Hey, you. Yes, you. How are you?

Let me tell you why we are here and why I wrote this book (because man, I can promise you - writing books is NOT easy). I wrote this book because I want to change your life. Bold statement, right? But I do, I really, really do.

You see, just a few years ago, my life was so completely different. I was tired, drained, stressed, riddled with self-doubt, low self-esteem and social anxiety. I often had THE worst thoughts (you know the ones I mean, right?). Then, from the depths of desperation, I saw a light. Literally. It was mental.

It was all down to ME.

I realised that there was one person that could change my life and that person was me. And only me. So, I went about gathering information, tools, techniques, exercises, qualifications, books, podcasts, journals - literally everything I could, to help me to work out what I could do to make the changes. It was life-changing. Often, when you realise how simple yet utterly transformational these things are, you just want to share them with as many people as possible. Why would you not want to? The world is a happier place when there are more happy people around.

It is natural to want to share. So, here is that sharing.

It is worth noting that there are thousands of people sharing things in their way and quite frankly, that's the best thing ever. There is room for us all. No one has a monopoly on sharing information that will make people happier! We tend to want to start with our family and friends because we all want our loved ones to be living their best lives, right? When we see how much they love it too, we want to share it with more and more people.

I won't be for everyone, and everyone isn't for me. Some of the most successful motivational speakers bore me to tears. And that's fine! In fact, it is brilliant, because it is what makes us all unique, interesting, brilliant and beautiful.

The point of this book is to give YOU some really simple tricks and techniques that you can use when you need a helping hand. Just a little pep talk, a pick-me-up, a one-woman vote of confidence. This book is here for you.

Keep it on your desk, your bedside table, your kitchen worktop, in your bag, in the downstairs loo, or on your phone (ebook style) and know that you can whip it out whenever you need a bit of a boost, a bit of pizazz or a zhoosh of energy.

Throughout this book, you will find secrets and tools that you can implement immediately that will change your whole way of being.

Over time, you will see that you start to do the techniques without thinking about them. You have created habits that support you. How amazing is that? I cannot wait for that to happen for you.

Then, perhaps you could give this book to your friend/nan/spouse/boss/neighbour/enemy/cat (delete as appropriate).

I am so glad you are here.

Enjoy the ride.

INTRODUCTION

Welcome, you wonderful, gorgeous, fabby, super human, you!

Firstly, I want to celebrate you for picking up this book and prioritising YOU for once. We have all heard the old 'put your own life jacket on first' analogy, but still, so few of us do. Between work, career, family and a million other responsibilities, we slide to the bottom of the priority heap, day after day after day. This is NOT good. It has to stop and it can stop.

It is not selfish to look after yourself, it is vital.

It is not lazy to take time out, it is necessary.

It is not egotistical to put yourself first, it is absolutely bloody brilliant!

And the way you can do it starts right here. Welcome to positive psychology - how you, and everyone you know, can benefit dramatically from consistently making a few simple changes to your life and your daily routine.

Happiness is your choice and your birthright, and it's coming right up.

HOW HAPPY ARE YOU?

You may have picked up this book because you believe that you are not living up to your potential in your personal or your professional life, or perhaps you are just not as happy as you hope to be.

The desire to be happier is felt by a huge proportion of the population, not just those who are clinically depressed. In the 'Happiness Survey, 2017'*, it was found that, at the most basic level, just 46% of people in the UK considered them-selves to be happy. That is less than HALF of the popula-tion. In this age of greater luxury, more travel, increased flexibility and independence; the population, in general, is not significantly happier than ever before. And it has to be noted here, this was pre-pandemic.

The conclusions of this study are listed below. These find-ings are perfect to share here because they completely

align with the messages, suggestions, techniques and tools
that I have highlighted in this book.

- Money isn't the key to happiness,
- People are more likely to feel happy on a healthy
  diet,
- People who exercise are happier,
- A job you enjoy will make you happier,
- Many people diagnosed with a mental health
  condition describe themselves as happy,
- Consistent solid sleep will improve your mood.

EAT WELL, SLEEP WELL, EXERCISE, ENJOY YOUR JOB. EASY, RIGHT?

These may seem to be quite obvious to you. Eat well, sleep
well, exercise, get a job you love and you'll be happier - job
done, right?

I cannot tell you the number of people who come to work
with me and, on the face of it, are wildly successful. They
may have a lovely house, holidays, a great (supposedly
satisfying) career, stability, happy healthy family - but there
is a huge void where happiness should be. When we work
our way through this list, there is HUGE room for improve-
ment. This is a good thing though because it means there is

so much they can do to change their situation to become happier, and happier, and happier!

IT'S OK TO GET AWAY

I have a little secret - you will never guess what; I started writing this book next to the glittering turquoise sea in the beautiful village of Cala Millor in Spain. I'm here on my own. Yes, you heard that correctly, I am in Spain, on my own! I can't quite believe it either. It is the first time I have been abroad since the big C changed everything in March 2020. It is the first time I have been abroad without the children. It is the first time I have been away on my own since having children twelve years ago! And it is absolutely brilliant. It sounds a bit entitled as I write this, but it wasn't easy to do.

When the idea first occurred to me to book a writing weekend somewhere warm and inspiring, I had absolutely no faith I would actually do it. Even after I booked and paid for it (less than 48 hours before departure!), I was wracked with guilt (I refuse to call it 'mum guilt' as that just gives strength to the narrative that mums should feel guilty if, god forbid, they ever have the audacity to think they can do anything that serves them). I was a little anxious about travelling in the post-covid era, the flight times were crazy (hence the bargain!) and I run two businesses - you know, stuff happens.

As you have read, I did indeed make it. And here I am. 'Why is this relevant?', you are probably thinking. It is entirely relevant to everything in this book. We need to have some time on our own every now and again to create some peace and make space to think and breathe. We need to value ourselves enough to think that we are worthy of a 'treat'. We need time and space to do the work that we are passionate about. We need to be able to pursue the work that makes us feel accomplished. We need to be valued and respected enough by our partners, families and loved ones for them to acknowledge that everyone benefits from a break, a change of pace and a change of scene.

THE 'ONE-UPMANSHIP' OF MARTYRDOM

Also known as the 'busyness badge of honour', we all seem to spend our entire lives trying to make out just how much busier we are than the next person. Busyness is used as an excuse for absolutely everything.

Late? "I am so busy and I only just managed to make it here."

Disorganised? "OMG, I am so sorry, I just have so much on and am SO busy ..."

Forgotten date/birthday/event - "I have been CRAZY busy this week and I just don't know what happened to my brain."

We have all been there, haven't we? We have found ourselves using these phrases and it feels awful. No one likes it. We hate letting people down yet still, we buy into this persona of insane busyness.

We have recently started to see time out as a weakness. I don't know what kind of Tom Foolery ever promoted this opinion, but seriously? How did we get to a point where society has reframed the BEST thing in life to something that we should be ashamed of taking? Literally ashamed. I once listened to a conversation where one of my friends was literally boasting about how long it was since they'd had a day off! 'I haven't taken a day off for three years, six months and twenty-six days and I'm not planning on taking one any time soon'! As though not being able to take a day off makes us somehow more important than other people? More indispensable? More special?

The effect? We stepped further and further away from taking this vital time out. We saw others around us working longer and longer days and thought that we should do the same. When people we knew told us they were going away for the weekend, we looked at them with feigned pity and said 'I don't know how you can manage, I just have way too much on' with that air of unspoken superiority. We've done ourselves a MASSIVE injustice.

WHAT CAN YOU DO?

Start small and simple - you could book a day off each month. Maybe you could read all day long, go for a really long walk, or a swim, or even do absolutely nothing at all.

We have to be as disciplined with our time off as we do with our work. It often helps to make a six-month plan. Could you include three weekends away? This gives you plenty of time to organise childcare, pet sitters, house sitters... whatever it is you need. This will make it far more likely that you really enjoy your time out.

Your time out will be completely unique to you. On my days off, I go for really, really long walks - maybe six or seven hours. Sometimes, I go for a spa day, sometimes, I get the car valeted, sometimes, I meet a friend for a walk and a long lunch and sometimes, I go for a massage. How often you can do this will entirely depend on your circum-stances. If you can't manage one day a month, try for a day every two months. Just start. The beauty of it is that your whole family will benefit. A healthier, happier, more content version of you is just around the corner. It really is.

21

THE HUSTLE IS OVER

Our mental health and well-being is just as important as our physical body and in some ways, more important. When we take care of our well-being, we provide a strong foundation for our lives. How many times do you go to the gym, go for a run or go to yoga class? Regularly, right? That's amazing. Your physical body is being well taken care of and that is so important. Now, it is time to give equal love and attention to your well-being - your mental health and your soul.

For decades, we have been told how important it is to stay fit and healthy, but the vast majority of this advice has revolved around diet and exercise. There has been a huge 'mind' shaped hole. The advice around looking after the well-being of your mind has always been way down the list of priorities. It has been seen as a 'nice to have', and touchy-feely. It has become apparent, however, in this post-lockdown era, that it is more important than ever to prioritise the health of our minds. After all, what good to you is a healthy and fit body, when you don't feel well in your mind?

It has always baffled me... we take care of our cars, our carpets, our leather sofas... we even polish our shoes! We take care of our pets, we prioritise the well-being needs of our children and teenagers, yet it is somehow seen as a weakness, or a luxury, an indulgence, to really spend time, investment and energy, on our own mental well-being?! Crazy, right?

Well, not anymore. It really does give me hope that the world is waking up to prioritising our well-being. Even positive psychology, which is known as the science of happiness or well-being, is a relatively new science. The internet is awash with images of self-care, and social media provides a great platform for sharing what we can do to support ourselves and improve our own happiness.

WHAT DETERMINES HAPPINESS?

This is quite possibly one of the most powerful things that you will ever learn. Did you know that you have control of around 40 per cent of your own happiness? How amazing is that?

It is widely understood that our level of 'happiness' can be determined as follows:

50% is your genetic set point/how you're made.

10% is your life circumstances and what you've been through.

40% is INTENTIONAL ACTIVITY - this is the part that you have control of!

This is the part we commonly call 'mindset'. We get to choose our own mindset. Realising this is the most important thing you will ever learn. The rest is down to you.

WHAT DETERMINES HAPPINESS?

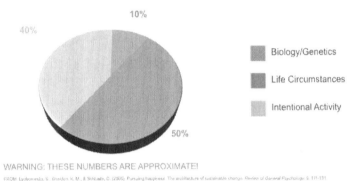

10%

40%

Biology/Genetics

Life Circumstances

Intentional Activity

50%

WARNING: THESE NUMBERS ARE APPROXIMATE!

FROM Lyubomirsky, S. Sheldon, K. M., & Schkade, D. (2005). Pursuing happiness: The architecture of sustainable change. Review of General Psychology, 9, 111-131.

HOW THIS BOOK WORKS

This book has been written and designed for you to carry around with you - in your bag, on your desk, on your bedside table, in your suitcase or on the coffee table... wherever works for you, then, when you encounter a situation that challenges you, you can whip it out and find out what you can do to help yourself in that moment.

There are exercises, tools, techniques and visualisations. They don't take long, they can be done wherever you are and can become your permanent companions in your times of need. Once you become familiar with the exercises, you can gift this book to someone else who you think might benefit from it. These exercises are great for all ages - children who have school anxiety, teens who need to cope with exam stress and young adults who need something to help them face university and job interviews. Once you have found the exercises that work best for you, you can also share them with your own friends and family so they can use them to improve their happiness too. Believe me, when you realise how different it feels to wake up excited, happy and hopeful every day, you WILL want to share it with those around you.

The ripple effect is an incredible thing. When we start to feel more positive, happy, content and joyful, this feeling spreads very quickly and effectively to those around us. Our friends and family also benefit and they start to feel the uplift too. Imagine that! Then the people they come into contact with also notice the change in them and that improves their lives too. We have the opportunity to change so many people's lives by radiating joy. Who wouldn't choose to do that?

WHY IT IS GOOD TO BE AN OPTIMIST

- Optimists experience less distress than pessimists when dealing with difficulties in their lives,

- Optimists adapt better to negative events (including life-threatening illnesses),
- Optimism protects new mothers against developing depression following the birth of the baby,
- Optimism is conducive to problem-focused coping, humour, making plans, positive reframing and accepting reality,
- Optimists don't ignore threats to their well-being,
- Optimists exert more continuous effort and tend not to give up,
- Optimists report more health-promoting behaviours,
- Optimists are more productive in the workplace.

Can optimism be learnt? YES!

HOW TO USE THIS BOOK

It is organised into the following chapters:

1. Self-confidence

2. Calm

3. Mood booster

4. Focus

5. Courage

6. Relationships

7. Fun

Read the book from start to finish, so you begin to understand the power of positive psychology and how we do have complete control of our own happiness.

You will find that some of the areas, topics, exercises and examples will really resonate with you. Make a mental note of these.

Have the book to hand over the space of a few weeks, and reach for it whenever you feel you might benefit from one of the sections.

Keep doing this.

This is what we call 'habit stacking'. It means that the more you introduce positive habits that enhance your well-being, the more you will get into the habit of taking actions that serve you, rather than actions that do not serve you.

Each chapter contains the following:

- An explanation of the topic,
- Exercise or intervention tool,
- Case study,
- Conclusion,

- Useful mantra.

As you work your way through the book, you will be able to identify the common themes that affect all areas of our lives. These include the way we talk to ourselves, who we interact with and how they impact us, how in touch we are with the way that we feel and how honest we are with ourselves about our feelings.

WHAT TO EXPECT

The pursuit of well-being is a fundamental human endeavour. We all strive to lead happy, healthy, and fulfilling lives but what exactly is well-being, and how can we achieve it? In this book, we explore the science of well-being, examining the latest research on the factors that contribute to our happiness and health.

We explore the concept of well-being and define what it means to be truly happy and healthy. We examine the different components of well-being, including physical health, mental health, social relationships and personal fulfilment. We also discuss the role of genetics and environmental factors in shaping our well-being.

We delve into the science of happiness, examining the latest research on what makes us happy. We explore the importance of positive emotions, such as joy, gratitude and contentment, as well as the role of negative emotions, such as anger and sadness. We also discuss the impact of external factors, such as income, on our happiness.

We explore the psychological factors that contribute to our well-being. We examine the importance of self-esteem, resilience and optimism in maintaining good mental health. We also discuss the role of mindfulness and meditation in reducing stress and promoting well-being.

We examine the biological factors that contribute to our well-being. We explore the role of neurotransmitters, such as dopamine and serotonin, in regulating mood and emotions. We also discuss the importance of exercise and nutrition in promoting physical and mental health.

We look at the social factors that contribute to our well-being. We explore the importance of social support, social connection, positive energisers and social integration in promoting mental and physical health. We also discuss the impact of social media on our well-being.

The importance of personal fulfilment and the pursuit of meaning and purpose are vital parts of how we feel. We examine the role of goals and values in shaping our lives and promoting well-being. We will also discuss the impact of work and career on our well-being.

Throughout the book, you will find practical strategies for enhancing well-being. We discuss the importance of self-care, including exercise, nutrition and sleep, as well as the role of mindfulness, meditation and other relaxation techniques in reducing stress and supporting our well-being. Finally, we discuss the importance of social support and community engagement in maintaining good mental and physical health.

The various interventions and practical strategies for enhancing well-being, including self-care, mindfulness and social support have been chosen specifically to support that particular aspect of the book. The overall aim is that by having a deeper understanding of the science of well-being, we can all work to lead happier, healthier and more fulfilling lives.

MANTRAS

You may be someone who is used to using mantras regularly, or you may be someone that thinks they're only for weirdos who also hug trees. Either is fine. We are all welcome here.

What mantras are good for, is helping create new neural pathways that support our well-being. They can replace the old patterns, the learned behaviours, the self-sabotage and the truly crappy habits that we have developed over the years for one reason or another, with strong, supportive, fabulous and fun lifestyle traits.

For example, since my children were small, we have chanted this mantra every morning on the way to school.

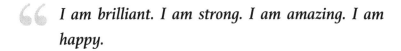 *I am brilliant. I am strong. I am amazing. I am happy.*

Some days they love it and chant with gusto; other days, they moan, eye roll and ask me why I can't be a normal mama. It's all swings and roundabouts, eh?

WHAT IS POSITIVE PSYCHOLOGY?

You will hear me refer to positive psychology a lot over the next few hours of your life, so I think I need to give you a mini explanation of what it is, how I came across it and why it is so relevant and important to us all.

BE THE DRIVER, NOT THE PASSENGER

Positive psychology is the study of optimal human functioning, what makes life worth living and better still, what we can do ourselves to make our own lives more amazing, more fun and more joyful. It was my own journey of life's ups and downs, and the subsequent realisation that I could be the driver, not the passenger, that piqued my interest. When I discovered that positive psychology was a science and that all of the interventions and exercises had been scientifically researched and tested, I became truly committed to finding out more.

Researching what goes well for individuals, communities and organisations is every bit as important to us as understanding what goes wrong. As a science, it focuses on discovering the empirical evidence for thriving. The vast majority of psychology, over the last forty years, has focussed on what is wrong with people and how to fix it. Anxiety, depression, low self-esteem and PTSD, and how these conditions can be improved for the individual have been the domain of applied psychology.

What I love about positive psychology is that it totally focuses on what we are amazing at and how to make the most of that in our lives and work. It doesn't try to fix what society perceives to be wrong with us, or what might be perceived that we are not good enough at.

As a society, we are in a much better place of accepting that we are all different and that we don't all necessarily have to fit into the same mould, so it makes sense that these changes are occurring now. Admittedly, society is still entirely set up to serve those of us who sit firmly within the neurotypical scale, but it does feel as though there is a shift towards accommodating different ways of being, working and thriving.

The most amazing aspect of working as a positive psychology coach is that my work is all about *applying* the science to real life. Some of the common conversation questions with my clients may be: How can we improve things? What do we need to do to support you in this situation? What is bringing you down and how can we change that? The combination of positive psychology and coaching psychology is so powerful because it literally creates a blueprint for an individual to thrive in their personal life, business or career and in their relationships.

IS THIS BOOK HELPFUL FOR NEURODIVERGENT INDIVIDUALS?

Yes, yes and yes again. My two children are both neurodivergent (ND) babes and, as I will explain in more detail later in the book, this was a major driver for me to start studying positive psychology. Strengths theory is particularly relevant for anyone with autism or ADHD because it asks the perfect ND question: what are you really good at and what do you love doing? And how can we make sure you do as much of that as possible in your life? Bingo!

I am no ND expert but I am a mum with lived experience and I am so grateful for the opportunities that strengths theory and positive emotions exercises have gifted us as a family. Tools such as the Feelings Wheel have transformed the quality of our communication immeasurably.

THE BITS ABOUT ME

The Little Book of Positivity is a combination of my learnings, snippets of my experiences and some anecdotal story-telling of the way I have applied positivity to my life. My own experiences are all told from my perspective and I have chosen to include them because this is my lived experience. This book is definitely not an autobiography (I have a lot of living to do yet!), but rather a little insight into what led me down the path of the pursuit of well-being.

I have seen so many life-altering transformations through my coaching work that it really drives me to want to change the way we approach our well-being. We don't have to be a passive patient, waiting for the next thing to be diagnosed or prescribed. Instead, we can take responsibility and ownership and do everything we can to make sure we are supporting ourselves in the best way possible.

I have included quite a few personal stories, experiences and anecdotes throughout the book because a) I am a chronic over-sharer and b) I want you to know there is absolutely no judgement here. I have made huge mistakes along the way, and if I share some of those with you, I hope that perhaps, you may be able to let go of any shame you may be feeling about yourself. I love hearing other people's stories. I find them fascinating, educational and so inspiring, but I have already admitted to being a nosey old trout, so I guess that comes as no surprise!

When I decided to stop drinking alcohol in 2019, I crammed my head full of other people's stories to remind myself why I was doing it. Some of the stories bore no relevance to my own experience but I still found them incredibly inspiring. I just wanted to hear stories of people, normal people like me, who had made big decisions and changes to support themselves to feel happier and healthier. I even launched a podcast because I had listened to everything available and wanted to hear more! (You can find *The Sober Stories podcast* on all podcast platforms.)

I vowed to myself at that time, that I would also share my story to help inspire others in the way that other people had inspired me. I was so grateful to all those people who were vulnerable enough to share their truth and I wanted to repay my thanks by offering mine too.

IF YOU'RE NOT CHANGING, YOU'RE CHOOSING.

This book is the first step to making those changes that YOU want to make. Whatever they may be, you deserve them, and you can do this. Living your life by intention will only ever be a good thing, and I am so utterly grateful to be part of that journey.

I want you to feel amazing, I want your kids to feel amazing, I want their kids to feel amazing. It is possible. Your story starts here.

USEFUL MANTRA

I am me. I celebrate me. I honour me and I respect me.

66 **The more grateful I am, the more beauty I see.**

— MARY DAVIS

HOW TO RAISE YOUR VIBRATION EVERY DAY

 Energy cannot be destroyed: it can only be changed from one form to another.

— ALBERT EINSTEIN

EVERYTHING IS ENERGY

If there is only one thing that I would like you to take away from this book, it is very clear, it's the most important thing of all - it is gratitude.

GRATITUDE

Make friends with gratitude.

We hear it all the time now as a well-being buzzword, which is absolutely amazing. When we feel grateful, we really have to feel it, through every part of our body, on a cellular level. I want you to get so used to feeling grateful that it exudes from you and becomes the very nature of who you are.

Did you know that it is impossible to feel grateful and negative at the same time? So, for every second we spend feeling grateful, we allow less negativity into our lives.

Even when it doesn't feel like it, we have so much to be grateful for. Sometimes, my gratitude is for the simplest things: a cup of tea, my dog, my trainers.

I am grateful for ...

> **When I started counting my blessings, my whole life turned around.**

— WILLIE NELSON

1

SELF CONFIDENCE

 'No one can make you feel inferior without your consent.'

— ELEANOR ROOSEVELT

What is confidence? My definition of confidence is not that you believe in yourself. It is more simple than that. You will believe in yourself if you start doing what I'm about to tell you. I absolutely LOVE this definition.

Confidence is the *willingness to try*.

The best thing is - everyone can learn to be more confident. That's right, absolutely everyone. That includes you!

It is the willingness to take action, even when it's not perfect. It's the willingness to speak in a meeting, even if you are worried you might sound stupid. It's to ask for what you deserve, even if you know you might be told no. It's the willingness to try something, even though you know you might not get it right. This willingness, in a moment of hesitation, to push yourself to take action, is the building block to changing absolutely everything. And the best thing? It is a skill that *you* can work on and develop. It is the secret to changing everything.

 "Those who have a 'why' to live, can bear almost any 'how"

— VIKTOR E. FRANKL

The most exciting thing about confidence is that everyone can learn it. Literally everyone. I'm not, for a second diminishing those who have crushing anxiety or those who doubt everything about themselves. I get it. It is a truly horrible feeling. But here's the thing; I know so many people who used to be like that but aren't anymore. They were desperate to change; desperate to work out how to be more confident and to dread social situations a little less, so, they learnt a set of techniques to enable them to overcome it.

At first, it may feel ridiculous, as if you are acting as a confident person when in actual fact, the total opposite is the case. The first time we do something new, it is often scary. We feel full of nerves, our stomach goes funny, our throats dry up - this happens to so many of us. However, when you have done something two or three times, it begins to feel easier and easier. Sometimes, the most important thing we can do is just go for it. We often wonder what we were worried about and why we hadn't started sooner!

ANXIETY: 'THE HABIT OF WORRYING SPIRALLED OUT OF CONTROL'

A habit is a pattern of behaviour or thinking that you repeat without realising it. Anxiety happens when the pattern of worrying about things spirals out of control and manifests itself with physical and psychological symptoms such as shallow breathing, headaches, tiredness or shaking. Anxiety is a feeling of worry, nervousness or unease about something with an uncertain outcome or an imminent event. It is a natural response to stress, but it can become problematic when it becomes excessive or persistent and interferes with daily life.

When we begin to look at our own habits, we can start to rebuild them and stack habits that support the way we feel.

It is a journey and may be hard work, but it is so worthwhile.

BE THE YOU YOU WANT TO BE RIGHT NOW

You've all heard of the phrase, 'Fake It Until You Make It', right? Well, this is not that! In fact, it is the exact opposite. This is about being the YOU you want to be – all the time, starting from right now.

We are taught, from a very young age, to do as we are told. At nursery, school, university, work, in society... everywhere. Slowly, but surely, the ability to put our head above the parapet and say, 'actually, that's not what I want to do', is ground down until it's not there at all.

 'Instead of trying to convince others you fit in their world, build your own'.

— NATALIE LOPEZ

IT STARTS WITH YOU

How amazing do you feel when you're all dressed up for a special event - a wedding or a ball? You feel a million dollars. You walk differently and when you glance at yourself in the mirror, you smile.

How do you feel when you're in sweatpants and a hoodie? You kind of curl up and hide in your own cosy bubble. Which is lovely, when kept in moderation (believe me, this is a good look for writing!). Then, you have to pop out - to pick something up, collect a parcel - and you bump into someone you know. How do you feel now? Aren't you wishing you'd put on your smart jeans and top? It has nothing to do with the other person either. It's all about the way you feel about yourself.

WHAT WOULD MORE CONFIDENCE MEAN TO YOU?

What would you do tomorrow if you had more confidence? Would you apply for a different, higher-paid job? Would you ask for a pay rise? Would you start your own business? Would you ask someone out? Would you tell your partner your sexual fantasies? Would you tell your neighbour to turn their music down? Would you tell your children to reach for the stars? Would you stop your anxiety medication? Would you quit your job and travel the world?

Would you do anything differently at all?

If the answer is no, you wouldn't do anything differently, let me tell you, you are most definitely in the minority. The research shows that over 81 per cent of people would make significant changes to more than one area of their life if they had the confidence. A huge number of those people would like to reduce their anxiety/depression medication but do not have the confidence to do it. They don't know what else to do so they just keep taking it.

What if more confidence meant fulfilling your wildest dreams? Is that something that sounds appealing to you?

When I begin working with people, they often start by saying that they are confident and they are happy with their confidence levels. They then go on to explain that they are on anxiety meds and they would love to change their job, move country, try a new hobby... but they're just not sure if they can do it, or whether they are good enough. People do not seem to connect being 'stuck' in their comfort zone as being related to low confidence, when, in actual fact, it is one and the same thing.

For most of us, more confidence would mean the willingness to try something that we don't feel able to at the moment, but that we would really like to. Imagine how it would feel to have the guts to just try the things you would love to do. When you see other people do amazing things and you think to yourself, I would love to do that but I don't think I can. I say this so many times in this book, but you only have one life. It is yours for the taking. I know you have it in you: you just need to believe that you do.

EXERCISE 1.1

CREATING CONFIDENCE WITHIN YOURSELF

Commitment. Consistency. Connection.

A Five-Minute Self-Esteem Exercise

This is a very powerful, confidence-boosting exercise that can be done in the moment to improve your confidence levels when you need a quick boost.

Many people use this exercise in the following circumstances:

- Before a date,
- Before a job interview,
- Before giving a presentation,
- Before confronting a challenging situation.

Take your notepad and pen:

1. Write down five of your strengths (These could be: a good listener, a loyal friend, a loving parent, calm, compassionate).
2. Take five deep breaths.
3. Write a sentence of gratitude for your strengths.
4. Take five deep breaths.

5. Acknowledge what you are scared of in the moment and write it down.
6. Take five deep breaths.
7. Repeat your list of strengths ten times out loud.

EXAMPLE

I am funny, I am a loving parent, I am patient at work, I am easy to talk to, I am kind to animals.

I am grateful that I am all of these things.

POSITIVE PROVERBS

These have become the fabric of society and are often bandied around culturally, without much real thought being given to the true meaning and power behind them. There are thousands of centuries of wisdom in some of these proverbs, so it is well worthwhile giving them some real time and space.

We may see them turned into wall art or memes, but do we truly think about the messaging behind them? There is so much hope and resilience in these proverbs. There are millions of people who have gone before us and have learned lessons that they want to pass on. We see, in these words, the ways in which humans want to share their knowledge and experience to make sure that future generations don't have to make the same mistakes that they made.

1. Failure is the mother of success.
2. When the sun rises, it rises for everyone.
3. Diligence is the mother of good luck.
4. The glory is not in never falling but in rising every time you fall.
5. Since the house is on fire, let us warm ourselves.
6. When one door closes, another one opens.
7. journey of a thousand miles begins with a single step.
8. Never worry worry - until worry worries you.
9. Laugh and the world laughs with you: cry and you cry alone.
10. A problem shared is a problem halved.
11. An ounce of prevention is worth a pound of cure.
12. Better to light a candle than curse the darkness.
13. Every cloud has a silver lining.
14. Count your blessings.
15. Forgive and forget.
16. Dig the well before you are thirsty.
17. Every beetle is a gazelle in the eyes of its mother.
18. We are born. We eat sweet potatoes. Then we die.
19. Success depends on your backbone, not your wishbone.
20. Where there's a will, there's a way.

21. Fortune favours the brave.
22. Procrastination is the thief of time.
23. Practise what you preach.
24. Practice makes perfect.
25. No one can make you feel inferior without your consent.
26. Imitation is the sincerest form of flattery.
27. Honesty is the best policy.
28. If at first, you don't succeed, try again.
29. Genius is one per cent inspiration, 99 per cent perspiration.
30. Failing to plan is planning to fail.

CASE STUDY: SELF-CONFIDENCE

Tim came to me because he had seen me talk at a local event and felt really inspired. He hoped that I could help him. Tim had been a plumber for fifteen years and had recently launched a much larger company, offering commercial solutions covering electrical, plumbing and renewables, and had a large team. His ambition was great, his self-belief less so. He was no longer 'on the tools' and instead, was a businessman who attended networking, corporate meetings and lunches. He had begun to feel so nervous before these meetings that it was affecting his performance. His vision and mission were very strong, but his patterns of behaviour were getting in his way.

'Who I am to walk in here wearing a suit? I've always been on the 'trades' and wearing work gear. Maybe I should forget all this and go back to what I have always done.'

Tim and I worked together over a few weeks and he started the 'five-minute self-esteem exercise' following our first session. The results were amazing. He did the practice every single morning and often in the evenings too - he was that committed to benefiting from the effects. He quickly began to realise that it was having a profound effect. The way he saw himself was changing, and he realised that he was just as valid as everyone else in the room/meeting/dinner and felt far more comfortable contributing to the conversation.

Interestingly, Tim recognised the value of this so much, that he has trained his whole team to use this exercise. This includes the office team, plumbers, electricians and senior leaders. He has invested in their well-being too because he knew how much difference it made to his own self image.

HOW TO APPLY THIS TOOL TO YOUR LIFE

There are two ways to use this tool.

The first is to familiarise yourself with the steps, then whip it out whenever you need it most. This may be a work meeting, a date, a public speaking engagement – whenever you feel you would benefit.

The second is to adopt it as part of a daily practice. This is so useful if you feel that you are battling with confidence generally (rather than in specific situations), as the repetitive practice will increase your confidence levels significantly over time.

WHO HAVE YOU ADMIRED?

One of the most effective ways to improve your confidence is to emulate those you admire. Have a think about people you have met over the last few years and those that stand out for you. It may have been a colleague, manager, friend, teacher or someone online that you really resonate with. Different people resonate with different people. That's what makes the world go round. So, have a think about what it is about this particular person that you admire. It could be their whole personality but sometimes, it is possible to break it down into specific aspects such as their voice, their style, their sense of presence, or even the colour of their nails! The reason that this works as an exercise is that it enables us to realise what specific aspects about people we admire.

When I started university in 1996, the first thing I did was join the choir (I know, I am SO rock 'n roll!). I was the only first year and many of the other choir society members were PhD students and staff so I spent all of the time in complete awe (I was very easily impressed back then, less so now!). There was one absolutely gorgeous woman called Victoria who I pretty much fell in love with as soon as I saw her. She was tall and floaty, with quite a serious air to her. She wafted into choir practice glamorously and I thought she was the best thing ever. She had just returned from a year in Paris and that made her even cooler. After one practice, she asked me if I wanted to go for a drink, and we went for a G&T in the student union bar. It was my first ever G&T (I used to drink back then!), and again, I was just bowled over by how utterly cool Victoria was.

To my delight, we immediately hit it off and we became great friends (she will roar with laughter when she reads this romantic account of our first meeting), however, meeting Victoria had been a fascinating learning experience for me. Basically, she curated the way she looked, spoke and acted. In other words, she had chosen the kind of impression that she wanted to give and she made that happen by the way she interacted with people, the way she dressed and how she carried herself.

To my amazement, Victoria hadn't always been this woman of poise and elegance. She had always been very short-sighted and had been bullied at senior school due to her thick glasses and general geekiness. She had struggled to make close friendships and felt very much as though she was an outsider. Just after finishing her A Levels, she read a book that changed her life. It was Dale Carnegie's, *How to Win Friends and Influence People*. After reading this book, Victoria realised that she was completely in control of the way she was perceived by others and found this to be the most liberating and exciting revelation! Victoria decided to change the way people saw her and made it happen. Her year in Paris enabled her to fine-tune the image that she wanted to create and she came back a different person. She described it as her contact lenses and silk scarf transformation because those were the things that had made the most difference.

I am telling the story of Victoria here for a particular reason. Victoria had no self-confidence and she wanted some. Victoria studied self-confidence and learned how to support herself in her quest for confidence and then, Victoria made it happen. We can all do this. It doesn't make us fake, it doesn't make us self-obsessed. It makes us the kind of person who has taken control of their own destiny and made it work in exactly the way we want it to. Surely, that just makes perfect sense.

I also spent an academic year in Paris. I studied at the Sorbonne Paris IV and lived near the steps of Montmartre. I wore a floor-length cashmere coat and thermal underwear because Paris is freezing!

It was the most wonderful time and it shattered another of the long-held beliefs that I had about people. I thought that being focused on physical appearance made people shallow and fake. I thought it meant that people were not clever and interesting. Paris smashed these judgements to pieces. Everyone I met was glamorous, from the university lecturer to the bus driver, and the street artist to the police.

HOW TO CURATE YOUR OWN CONFIDENCE

I recently listened to an interview with the actor Brian Blessed. Brian is famous for his voice. His voice is his USP and it is what has secured him the vast majority of his work over the years. He has a deep, resonating tone with beautiful pronunciation and he is very well-spoken. The interviewer asked Brian if he had always had this beautiful smooth voice, and Brian erupted into laughter. 'Of course not,' he said, 'This voice is the result of fifty years of hard work and fine-tuning'. Brian went on to explain that he worked on his voice for an hour and a half, every single DAY! He likened it to practising an instrument and putting in the hours to ensure that his instrument was performing at peak level.

I chose to mention this specific example because I am contacted by a lot of people who don't like their voice. Some don't like their accent, others don't like the pitch or the tone of their voice, and this affects their confidence. Be like Brian Blessed and change it to a voice that you do want and that will make you confident! It is your voice and you can do what you like with it.

The same can be said for your body, your hair, your skin, your clothes and anything else about you. It is entirely down to you to choose what will make you feel the most self-confident you can feel. And that is exciting.

EXERCISE 1.2

GIVE YOURSELF A HIGH FIVE IN THE MIRROR. EVERY SINGLE DAY

Louise Hay wrote *You Can Heal Your Life,* way back in 1984. (By the way, this is the book that changed my life more than any other – details in the bibliography). In her book, she asks us (the readers) to do 'mirror work'. Every single morning, you look in the mirror, look directly into your own eyes and say:

 'Faye (insert your name here, don't use mine!), I love and accept you exactly as you are.'

THE LITTLE BOOK OF POSITIVITY

The amazing Mel Robbins wrote the fantastic *The High Five Habit,* in 2021. The premise is that we give ourselves a high five in the mirror every single morning. And in the evening if you fancy it. And at any other time you feel the need.

Mirrorwork is very powerful. Once you get over feeling like an absolute fool – don't worry, we all do the first few times – it becomes a wonderful habit. Also, what is that all about? Why on earth would we feel a fool in our own bathroom, with no one else there?

Quite often, this work can bring about big shifts. Think about it, we spend so much of our time looking in the mirror and beating ourselves up.

I look old.

I look tired.

My eyes are puffy.

I have wrinkles.

I look too fat/thin/tall/short...

Imagine if we stopped that completely. If we look ourselves straight in the eye and make a positive declaration, give ourselves a high five and start to smile.

I love and accept you exactly as you are.

I am an amazing friend.

I am a wonderful parent/sibling/cousin.

I love my body for serving me in the way that it does.

It is these small but MIGHTY changes that, over time, once we commit to them, really do change our lives.

Take some post-it notes and stick them all over your bathroom mirror. Write wonderful, uplifting and complimentary phrases on each one. Each time you look in the mirror, you will be giving yourself a little TED talk about how amazing you are.

EXERCISE 1.3

FIND YOUR HALF-SMILE

When you look at an image of the happy Buddha, you will often see him with a tranquil, half-smile on his face. The smile symbolises joy in the present and a total lack of ego.

When you find yourself in a moment that lacks joy, or perhaps you feel full of ego, for example, waiting in line or in a business meeting, try and adopt a half-smile. As you breathe in, feel the corners of your mouth lift ever so slightly. Hold this half-smile for a few breaths as you relax into your positive present.

Having learnt about these three tools, you can now put them in your well-being toolkit and they sit there ready for whenever you need them. You may use them every day, or you may go through phases where you use them a lot, and then don't need them for a few days afterwards. Just knowing that you understand them and that they work, is going to make so much difference to the way that you feel about yourself.

This paragraph right here could quite possibly be the foundation to changing your life. Imagine that? It doesn't have to be difficult.

The most important thing to remember here is that we are not our past. Shy people can become confident. What you do with that depends on what YOU want.

Some may want to be confident enough to speak on a stage to thousands of people. Someone else may want to be confident enough to walk into a yoga class. Your story is your priority. You don't need to, and won't benefit from, comparing yourself to other people. Get really clear on what confident looks like for you. If you feel you don't know what it looks like, take a paper and pen and start writing down what a confident you may look like. You will find the ideas start to flow and before long, you will have so much more clarity.

Confidence is a skill that can be built upon. It doesn't matter where you have been, it doesn't matter what your preset for confidence was when you were born, it doesn't matter what you have endured in your past, confidence is a skill that you can build using simple, repetitive tasks and thinking tools. You can start building it today using the tools we have shared in this chapter. I know you can do it.

USEFUL MANTRA

I am brilliant. I am strong. I am amazing. I am capable.

2

CALM

> "*Holding onto anger is like grasping a hot coal with the intention of throwing it at someone else: you are the one getting burned.*"
>
> — BUDDHA

What do you do in a drama or a crisis? Are you the one that everyone turns to for a rational, calm, reasoned response? Or do you struggle to keep perspective and feel overwhelmed and stressed?

Think of the people you know. Who would you describe as calm? How do they respond to things? What is it about their behaviour that you would like to experience too? How

59

do you think it would benefit your life to be calmer? In what ways do you see life improving if things were calmer?

CALM, OR LESS STRESSED?

I was going to call this chapter, 'How to not be stressed' because dealing with stress is quite possibly the biggest threat to our well-being. When people are struggling, we look to stress as the reason. We know that stress can cause havoc with our physical body. There are actual physiological changes that occur as a result of stress.

What has become clear, however, is that we often refer to the regular day-to-day happenings of life as 'stress'. The things that happen in our lives become the source of our stress. Our work, health, family, finances - these are not stress, this is life itself. When we frame them as stress, we have indicated to ourselves that we are not able to cope with the things that are happening to us. We are never going to be able to remove 'life', therefore, we are never going to be able to remove 'stress'. So, what is actually going on here? When did life become stress?

Just for a second, have a think about humanity. Was there ever a time that humans didn't have to cope with the following?

- Illness,
- Tragedy,
- Death,
- Scarcity,
- Danger,
- Grief,
- Loss.

Humans have had to deal with all of these things since the dawn of time. We have always had to work, to find food, raise our young, protect ourselves, build shelter and keep ourselves safe. These are the aspects of being a human that have always existed. The modern world has designed a huge variety of devices and contraptions that are supposed to make our lives easier but which, in reality, contribute to more stress.

Worry is thinking about unpleasant things that might happen. Stress is a mental tension that causes a physical reaction in your body. When you are stressed, adrenaline is released into the bloodstream to speed up your reactions. Blood is then sent from the skin to your muscles to give them extra power and enable them to move quickly. This 'fight, flight or freeze' response was useful to our ancestors (who may, for example, have had to escape from huge predators), but leaves us feeling irritable and shaky as there has been no physical release.

HOW TO REFRAME

Reframing is one of the most powerful mindset and positivity tools we can ever have in our arsenal of handy go-to toolkits. We are socially conditioned to perceive things in a certain way and, as with everything, it is totally within our power to decide to perceive things in a different way.

We just have to break free!

Reframing enables us to do this. We can take a situation that we may automatically have seen as negative and instead look at what we might be able to take from it that makes it a positive experience. Reframing is one of the most important life skills we can develop. It is super contagious so we can pass on our wonderful, golden energy to those around us.

JUST SAY NO

We are all just so busy these days. It is an accepted part of life in the 21st century. How often do you chat with colleagues or family members, only for them to tell you that they are just so, so busy? It's the modern-day affliction. We seem to have arrived at a place where our self-worth and importance are measured by how busy we are. Am I important? Well, I must be busy to prove that.

The thing is, being busy is stressful. It contributes to chaos and feeling rushed and stressed. It does not contribute to a calm life at all. There is a fine balance between doing all the things that you enjoy and want to do in life, and being so rushed off your feet that you don't have time to savour the moment, or spend true quality time with your family. This impacts your well-being, which impacts your relationships, which impacts your well-being even further. You can see what is happening here; it is a downward spiral that is not serving you at all.

One of the main reasons that we end up too busy, is that we do not have the ability to be able to say no to things that we don't have the time for. This could be at work, but may also be in voluntary roles, or helping and supporting family and friends. At some point in recent history, it was decided that saying no was bad manners. We became a society of people pleasers and felt too bad to turn stuff down, even when we didn't have the capacity to take it on. As a result, we end up saying yes to everything we are asked to do, and end up way too busy to do anything properly, which makes us stressed.

DO YOU NEED TO GET BETTER AT SAYING NO?

Have you found yourself in a position where you have said yes to things you just don't have the time for?

Do not beat yourself up. This situation comes from trying to be kind to others... and ending up being not-so-kind to yourself. Instead, have a really honest conversation with yourself about what you DO enjoy, and which of those things that you DO have time for. You will end up with a wonderful list of things you want to do and can devote yourself to.

The same applies in work, though many of us find it even more difficult to have boundaries in our professional lives. It is scientifically proven that people who exercise boundaries at work are respected more by their peers and their managers. It also shows that the quality of their work is better.

ONE-UPMANSHIP OF MARTYRDOM

When I first moved to Cornwall, many of the mums I met were either farmers or married to farmers. They lived in exquisite places with rolling acres of fields and woodland, yet they were all absolutely run ragged most of the time. I was visiting one of these friends on her beautiful farm in 2017. I was having a conversation with her husband and another friend of his, who was also a local farmer. This is how the conversation went:

Farmer 1: "How are you? Busy, yes busy, I haven't had a day off in over two years."

Farmer 2: "Two years! Easy for some. I haven't had a day off in over three and a half years!"

I nearly fell over. These guys were using their busyness as a badge of honour. They were using it to metaphorically joust with each other about who was the most important. It was all in good humour, but the undercurrent was that it was cool to be busier. I began to realise that we all do that, to a certain extent, and we all feel we have to make out that our situation is tougher than everyone else's. It has become a one-upmanship of martyrdom.

It isn't only applicable to farmers. I see this all the time in all different walks of life. The online space is particularly bad for it due to the hustle culture.

If you can feel yourself being drawn into this, it can be really effective to do a short 'three good things' exercise (see exercise 3.3 later for more about this). As always, no blame or judgement to our colleagues or family members who do still sit in this mentality - we just don't need to join them there.

OH, TO BE CALM

For many years, whenever I created vision boards, the word CALM was the centre of it all. I was craving calm. I didn't really know that I was until I did these vision boards.

At the time, I had two young children and a lively dog, I lived at my business, which was very much guest-facing, and there was zero downtime. Also, running a guest-facing business, there was very little holiday time. I was stressed, drained and pretty high vibe. I used to dive into my 'well-deserved' glass of wine in the evening, as that was my way to chill out. Only, it never quite hit the spot. If you're drinking to self-medicate, it very quickly loses any pleasure and becomes just that – a medicine.

In 2019, I made the decision to stop drinking alcohol. At the time, I didn't know how long for, but I just went with it. Immediately, a sense of calm descended. Softly and quietly at first, then slowly becoming more obvious and long-lasting. This chapter is not about giving up alcohol – that decision is a personal one. What I will suggest though, is that every single one of you go alcohol-free for one month per year. Dry January, Sober October – any other month in between... you decide. It's a great treat for your body, even if you don't drink very much.

THE PEOPLE AROUND YOU

Stress is a contagion and our responses to the events in our lives are significantly influenced by those around us. This means that the more drama we have in our friends and families, the more drama and stress we are likely to create.

We absorb the responses and behaviours of those around us over time and, without realising, our behaviour becomes closer and closer to others, even if we don't want it to. If you know people who are often moaning and bitter about people and life in general, you will notice that the rest of their families and friends may have that approach to life too.

Things like road rage, neighbour disputes, disagreements with colleagues: these behaviours are often based in anger that has come from an unresolved emotional issue. The issue will stay unresolved unless it is acknowledged and treated successfully, perhaps through therapy. However, the far more significant reach is on those around the person with the angry approach to life. This anger spreads quickly through close acquaintances, and children are particularly prone to absorbing this anger response to life.

 'I am healthy, whole and complete.'

If any of this behaviour sounds familiar, the best thing you can do for yourself is to distance yourself as much as possible from those exhibiting these behaviours. Our relationships form such a huge part of who we are and we therefore need to choose our influencing relationships so wisely.

This may not sound possible if the people described above are members of your close family, however, you will not be able to change them. Only they can choose to change themselves if they want to. Once you have distanced yourself from them, they will begin to notice a change in your behaviour and approach to life and this may well help them to start making similar changes for themselves.

In positive psychology, we recognise relationships as one of the six guiding pillars (PERMAH). Our relationships have a profound effect on our overall levels of happiness and joy. Many of the people I work with find this difficult because although they recognise that their family is often a source of negativity, anger and drama, they do not want to remove them from their lives (for obvious reasons!). Instead, we work together to bring more positive relationships INTO their lives. This is a great approach to relationships because we are able to bring more and more aligned people into our daily routines, which means we have a much healthier balance of influences surrounding us.

ENABLING UPLIFTING RELATIONSHIPS

The best way to bring aligned people into your life is to take up an aligned activity. This will be different for everyone but some examples are:

- Team sports,
- Crafting,
- Sailing,
- Fishing,
- Golf,
- Volunteering.

The list really could go on forever. When we introduce activities like this into our lives, the positive impact is twofold. One, we get to regularly enjoy an activity that we enjoy, and two, we get to meet other people who enjoy that same activity. We are far more likely to be aligned with people who choose the same activities in life, so this is often a source of wonderful, positive, uplifting relationships.

OUR DAILY ROUTINE

The other main area to focus on when we want to feel more calm, is our daily routine. Life itself can feel manic and chaotic. Family, work, children, hobbies - these can all contribute to life feeling the opposite of calm.

Try and introduce a daily routine that works for you and you will soon find that home life feels much calmer for everyone. If you have a family, you will know what a juggle daily life can be sometimes. Many children thrive on routine and it is helpful for them to know what to expect and when, so they feel comfortable in their surroundings.

I touch on this elsewhere in the book, but a morning routine is a great way to ensure you all start the day in a calm way. Simple steps such as making sure the kitchen is tidy in the evening, laying out clothes for the next day, and leaving plenty of time for contingency, all contribute towards a lovely morning.

I must caveat this with an honest mum perspective - our mornings are not all like this. We have frantic 'find-the-shoe' moments, we have last-minute homework, we have meltdowns and tantrums. To me, these things are all part and parcel of life and, if I'm honest, add a bit of colour and adventure along the way! We do, however, need a strong framework to make sure that we are not totally derailed when these things do happen. I don't know about you but I cannot stand being late. I have never liked the stress that it brings on and so would much rather be ridiculously early. I know that doesn't apply to all of us, but it is just my coping mechanism in this particular scenario. My children find it highly annoying and constantly give me grief for it, but I reckon they will secretly thank me one day!

EXERCISE 2.1

TAKE FIVE BREATHING - ONE OF THE MOST PROFOUND TOOLS YOU WILL EVER CARRY

1. Spread out the fingers of one hand,
2. Very slowly, begin to trace a finger up and down each finger on the other hand,
3. As your hand moves up, breathe in deeply through your nose,
4. As your hand reaches the top, hold the breath for three counts,
5. As you hand moves down, breathe out through your mouth and empty all the air,
6. Hold for three counts before moving onto the next finger,
7. Repeat for all fingers (and thumb!) and notice how much calmer and slower you feel.

HOW TO APPLY THIS TOOL TO YOUR LIFE

Take Five breathing is life-changing. You can literally do it whenever you need it - at work, on a date, in a traffic jam, before an interview, with your kids - the list is endless.

James Nestor, author of '*Breath: The New Science of a Lost Art*', explains, 'No matter what you eat, how much you exercise, how skinny or young or wise you are, none of it matters if you are not breathing properly. Nose-breathing plays a vital role in our health, one that we have underestimated for many years. Make sure you are breathing through your nose as much as possible during the day, it has a fantastic calming effect.'

STAYING CALM IN A CRISIS

I had just found out a friend had died. It was a tragic accident and my friend, at the time of their death, was just eighteen years old. I was momentarily stunned. And then, in an instant, I realised that I was needed. I began forming a plan and started taking action to get things in motion.

I read the eulogy at both of my grandparents' funerals. It was a great honour and I was so pleased that I was able to do that for them both. I didn't know much about specific breathing techniques at the time, but I knew that slow, purposeful, regular breathing helped me to stay calm and in control of my emotions. If I felt a wave of tears coming, I could take a deep breath, slowly hold it in, release it calmly, and I could feel the tears subside. I found this really empowering. There's nothing worse than crying uncontrollably when you really, really don't want to. It's a horrible, vulnerable feeling and can really affect us. So, having a tool to be able to control it, is really helpful.

Someone recently said to me 'well, you're obviously not as affected by things as I am'. I was aghast. How could they say that about me? I was really upset. As I began to think more about it, I realised why I had felt triggered by what they'd said. It was almost being suggested that I didn't have feelings. Was I heartless? Was I an uptight old trout? Thankfully, I was able to see the situation from their perspective and realised that it made them feel vulnerable about showing their feelings. There is nothing more disabling than being overwhelmed by uncontrollable feelings (when you don't want them!).

CASE STUDY: CALM

Lucy is a successful property developer in the UK. She contacted me as she was nervous about life. She had just become a single parent to three girls following her marriage ending. It was an amicable separation, thankfully, and she was philosophical about it and looking forward to the future.

Her concerns were more around being a mum, a property developer, dealing with tenants and guests, running a regular networking meeting and still having time for herself - to exercise, connect with friends and take part in her local hockey club.

We brainstormed the essential things in the diary, then added the desirable elements and figured out where she would need flexibility and support.

We listed who she could ask for support on a regular basis and how she would feel comfortable doing this. She contacted a number of school mums to ask them whether she could call on them if she ever needed to. Guess what? They all said yes!

We have to be vulnerable to be able to ask for help. For many of us, particularly if we are hyper-independent, it can feel like we may have failed in being able to manage on our own, however, it is vital to accept help to be able to thrive in all the areas that matter to you.

Lucy made some small but significant changes. She always cleaned and tidied the kitchen before bed, no matter how tired she was, so she came down to a fresh, clean start each day. She started getting up a little bit earlier each day to give herself time for some peace and quiet (and online yoga) before the children woke up.

She scheduled a daily walk into her diary thereby ticking off two of the LIFE list - fresh air and movement.

She checked her diary every evening so she knew what she, and the children, had scheduled the following day.

She kept a pen and notepad in her bedroom and scribbled down any thoughts she had before bed, so 'emptying' her brain of any swirling thoughts that might keep her awake.

FROM DISCIPLINE COMES THE GREATEST FREEDOM

Lucy was quite resistant at first, about having such a full diary, as she said she held freedom as one of her driving values - and this level of planning didn't feel like freedom. Once Lucy had started to get used to these new patterns, she thrived. She quickly began to see that the routine and structure were the framework and the foundation from which, the calm environment would come.

CREATING A CALM WEEK

A calm morning means a calm day. A calm day means a calm week. A calm week means a calm month. Calm months mean a calm life.

It is a step-by-step framework that has to start at the beginning. If you have a wild, frantic and chaotic morning every single day, the chances of you having a calm day are drastically reduced. I understand completely that none of us can guarantee a calm morning every single day, but what if we aim for most days? That is a huge step in the right direction.

Organisation and discipline are important factors in a calm morning. And before you go running to the hills, this does not mean being a control freak! It just means acknowledging the things that DO make you feel amazing in the morning and working out how you can make that happen consistently.

Let's be honest, we all want calm to a certain level, don't we? Calm doesn't mean boring. Calm means fun, easy, simple, flowing and joyful. When we make room for calm, the rest of the good stuff flows straight in. Many of us are hesitant to embrace organisation because we think it detracts from our life choices of, perhaps, freedom and autonomy. What it actually does, is create the time and space and mental energy that gives us freedom and clarity which, in turn, brings calm.

My calm life is wonderful for the following reasons:

- I am on time when I need to be,
- I can find things when I need them,
- I pay bills and invoices on time, which saves me stress,
- I remember birthdays (mainly!),

- I am showing my children, via role-modelling, that calm improves our day-to-day lives,
- I am in a better position to help and support my loved ones.

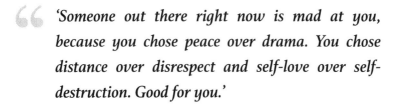 *'Someone out there right now is mad at you, because you chose peace over drama. You chose distance over disrespect and self-love over self-destruction. Good for you.'*

— ADAM CAM

EXERCISE 2.2

SAVOURING

Noticing and appreciating life's small and everyday occurrences is a really powerful tool for improving our wellbeing. We often spend so much of our modern lives rushing from one thing to the next that there is little time for savouring the actual thing we are in the middle of. In fact, what we can end up doing is rushing through the things we are doing to get on to the next thing we need to do, then, when we get to the next thing, we then rush through that to get to the next thing. Sounds crazy, right? But, alarmingly familiar too? Do not worry, you are not alone.

We hear an awful lot about the importance of being 'in the moment', but I wonder how many of us actually know what that really means.

Step 1: Make a drink of your choice,

Step 2: Sit down and do nothing else other than enjoy the drink,

Step 3: Savour each mouthful - note the taste, the temperature and the scent,

Step 4: Close your eyes and create some mental imagery of this moment,

Step 5: Absorb yourself. Try not to think, just sense and savour this moment.

WHY DOES THIS WORK?

This tool is so wonderfully simple because you can do it as often as you need. You can also do it wherever you are, when you know you just need to slip into a calm state. It doesn't have to be a drink, it could also be something to eat or a piece of music. The important part of this exercise is to create a moment where you are fully able to savour and stay with that feeling of savouring for as long as you can.

Appreciation crops up a lot in positive psychology and savouring can be seen as a more down-to-earth definition of appreciation. I find it really useful to think of this in all three senses of the word: to be thankful, to acknowledge the quality of something and to increase in value. Savouring is about really noticing, appreciating and enhancing the positive experiences in our lives. By savouring, we slow down and consciously pay attention to all of our senses.

A really great circuit breaker if you are feeling very anxious is to do a five-step sense test.

1. What can I see?
2. What can I hear?
3. What can I smell?
4. What can I touch?
5. What can I taste?

By the nature of doing this, we are fully brought back into the present moment and it can be highly effective to get us out of our busy heads and back into our body.

There is only good that comes from having a calm life. If we need more stimulation, we can include it by way of sports and hobbies. In fact, when our regular day-to-day lives are calmer, we have more time and space for hobbies, activities and sports.

Make intentional breathing a regular practice to calm yourself.

Introduce calming habits into your daily life.

Reject that narrative that we are all crazy busy all of the time – it doesn't have to be that way.

USEFUL MANTRA

I know when I am calm I feel better. I use my breathing to stay calm and focused.

3

MOOD BOOSTER

> 'Optimism isn't a passive expectation that things will get better; it's a conviction that we can make things better.'

— MELINDA GATES

What does optimism mean to you? Would you describe yourself as an optimist? Are you a cup-half-full, or half-empty, kind of person? According to Martin Seligman, godfather of positive psychology, anyone can learn optimism. When we have a more joyful outlook on life, we are in a much better position to enhance our own well-being. At work, for example, optimism is linked to an intrinsic motivation to work harder, to be able to endure stressful circumstances and to be able to focus on goals and achieve them successfully.

GLASS HALF-FULL OR HALF-EMPTY?

Have a think about the people you know. Who stands out as an optimist? There may be one person or a few people, but there is always someone you can think of. How does that person seem to you? Are they fun to be around? Do they seem to be joyful? How do you think they make their immediate family members feel?

I am sure you can see where I am going with this. You will also see this come up in various different ways in this book. What we put out, we attract back. If we are upbeat, hopeful and energetic, we attract those kinds of people back into our lives. That is why you often see groups of friends who all have the same bright and positive disposition.

This book doesn't really cover romantic relationships (as this is most definitely not my area of expertise!) but there are some incredible mood-based exercises we can do if we do want to see how we can impact our dating experiences. When working with clients, dating is often a hot topic because people often feel as though they repeatedly attract a similar kind of person. Put simply, if you come across as downtrodden, down-in-the-dumps, grumpy and generally critical of the world, you will more than likely attract a similar kind of person. It is really worth asking yourself if that is the kind of person you want to date. From this perspective, it can be very worthwhile to be introspective and exercise some honest self-awareness. It is never an easy task, but it can fundamentally change the vibrations that we put out to the rest of the world.

Please take this all with plenty of love (I have loads to go around), and know that dating can be an uplifting, fun and interesting experience (and experiment!). As with all things, there are exceptions to the rule, where the optimist falls in love with the world-weary grump, but I probably wouldn't recommend that as a strategy. Ultimately, no one ever needs to change for anyone else, but if you are here because you want to change for YOU, you're in the right place.

SUNSHINE AND ROSES?

While some may say that there are some downsides to being an optimist, they are outweighed significantly by the benefits, which are both physical and psychological. In fact, there are so many desirable characteristics linked to optimism that the benefits can dramatically change your life.

It is so incredibly important to note here that being optimistic is NOT denying your real feelings. It is not invalidating anyone else's real feelings and it is not blocking them out or brushing them under the carpet. Instead, I like to think of being optimistic as the underlying golden thread that enables you to realise that, no matter what happens, we are always able to handle it. We do have the strength and the fortitude within us to be able to handle it, whatever 'it' is.

In 2016, I read the most important book of my life, '*Feel the Fear and Do It Anyway*', by the wonderful Susan Jeffers. This is the one book I recommend absolutely everyone reads, no matter who you are, what your circumstances or what you want to achieve. This book was published in 1987 and is still as relevant today as it was the day it was written. Millions of people worldwide have benefited from the message Susan Jeffers was guided to share, which is this very simple message:

I can handle it.

WHY BE OPTIMISTIC?

- Optimists suffer less anxiety, depression and distress than pessimists,
- Optimism is linked to more effective coping,
- Optimistic people tend to deal with problems rather than avoid them, and use more acceptance, humour and positive reframing,

- Optimists travel more and are more embracing of different cultures, religions and traditions,
- Optimists make more money, have more friends, laugh more and experience more fulfilling relationships.

WHAT IF I'M NOT AN OPTIMIST?

This is a great question, and thankfully, the answer is also great! You can just become one. It is that simple.

The main reason any of us ever finds ourselves being pessimistic is because it is a behaviour that we have learned - from our families, our friends, our communities, our schools and our colleagues. We are repeatedly told to 'not get our hopes up', to 'manage expectations' and to 'be realistic' in our outlook and our approach to life. Over time, like most things we are told, we adopt this view of the world where we never feel we can get excited about things in case the thing we are excited about never happens.

Whaaaaat?! What lunacy is this?

Our thoughts become reality so BE EXCITED. Honestly, the more excited you get, the more likely it is that the amazing things we are excited about WILL happen. What we give out, we attract back. If we permanently tell

FAYE EDWARDES

ourselves that nothing good is going to happen, guess what? Nothing good will happen.

STEPS TO INCREASE OPTIMISM

Everyone experiences periods of low mood, whether it's due to a difficult life event or just a bad day, however, it is important to take steps to boost your mood and improve your mental well-being.

Exercise has been shown to boost your mood and reduce feelings of stress and anxiety. Even a short walk or a quick workout can release endorphins, which are natural mood boosters. Just thirty minutes of moderate exercise every day, whether it's a brisk walk, a yoga class, or a bike ride will be a huge mood boost.

Mindfulness is the practice of being present in the moment and focusing on your thoughts and feelings, without judgement. By practising mindfulness for just a few minutes each day, focusing on your breath and observing your thoughts and feelings without reacting to them, mindfulness meditation has been shown to reduce symptoms of depression and anxiety and increase feelings of well-being.

Social support is crucial for maintaining good mental health. There is so much evidence to show the positive impact of spending time with friends and family, and making an effort to connect with others, whether it's through volunteering, joining a club or taking a class. Surrounding yourself with positive, supportive people boosts your mood and provides a sense of belonging.

What you eat has a significant impact on your mood. Eating a balanced diet that includes plenty of fruit, vegetables, whole grains and lean protein can help stabilise your mood and reduce feelings of stress and anxiety. Avoid processed foods, sugary snacks and excessive amounts of caffeine, which can contribute to mood swings and feelings of irritability.

There is a strong and growing movement around the subject of gut health and how much it impacts the way that we feel. UPF (ultra-processed food) is linked with low mood, low energy, low sex drive and generally feeling down. According to Dr Tim Spector, author of *Food for Life: The New Science of Eating Well*, we need as many fresh vegetables as we can manage, every single day. He recommends aiming for thirty different types of fresh vegetables or grains to support our gut microbiomes. This includes seeds and nuts, but it is still a bit more than the old five-a-day that we have been used to hearing about. This makes perfect sense to me.

Do you ever find yourself craving crunchy, fresh and juicy fruit and vegetables? Our bodies cannot function without fresh food. So many of my clients are suffering from low energy and disrupted sleep, while also having huge amounts of processed food. Once we learn to truly support ourselves, we have a much better chance of avoiding a great amount of illness, chronic conditions and discomfort.

CHANGE YOUR MORNING, CHANGE YOUR LIFE

Lack of sleep can have a significant impact on mood and mental well-being. I studied the Miracle Morning routine and became a certified MM coach. *The Miracle Morning* is a book by Hal Elrod, which sets out a prescriptive morning routine that sets you up for an amazing day. Many people find it too rigid and incompatible with real life, but I loved it. I didn't ever follow the system to the letter, but I found it so inspiring to know that I could use my morning time *for* me and to create a fantastic start to my own days.

When I work with clients, I have found that the most effective way to improve sleep is for the client to consistently get up early. It sounds crazy, I know. Many people are resistant or simply feel that they cannot do it. However, a consistent wake-up time for at least two weeks will support a sleep reset attempt. It is vital to avoid screens and stimulating activities before bed and to create a calming environment in your bedroom. The definition of early is different for different people. I tend to wake up between 5.30 am and

6.00 am. This took me about six months of consistency to achieve. Early morning has been my absolute favourite time of day for over five years now and I wouldn't change it for the world. You will find that so many early risers say the same.

It is important to note here that so many people are so resistant to this. They are convinced that their body clock doesn't work that way and that they are much more of an evening person. On the one hand, yes, of course, I agree that we are all different. On the other, if you really are struggling with low-quality sleep, low energy and low mood, I would urge you to be open-minded and to give this a try because it has helped every single person I have ever worked with on it.

Focusing on what you're grateful for can help shift your mindset and improve your mood. Each day, write down a few things you're grateful for, whether it's a supportive friend, a beautiful sunset or a good book. By focusing on the positive aspects of your life, you can boost your mood and increase feelings of happiness and contentment.

By making small changes to your daily routine, such as exercising, practising mindfulness, connecting with others, eating a healthy diet, getting enough sleep and practising gratitude, you can improve your mental well-being and lift your spirits. Remember, it's important to prioritise your own needs and take care of your mental health in order to lead a happy, fulfilling life.

YOU'RE SO LUCKY, YOU ARE A BORN OPTIMIST

I do get this, don't get me wrong. I understand that some people just seem naturally chirpier than others. This makes it easy for the rest of us to say to ourselves, 'I just wasn't born that way. They are a born optimist, I am not.'

Many of you reading this book may say the same about me. I might be described as bubbly, happy and smiley, but I am no different from anyone else. There have been many times when I haven't felt any of those things. Instead, I have felt low, blue, hopeless and helpless. Sometimes, I choose to feel these feelings privately, which may give the impression to others that I am always chirpy.

No one is always chirpy and that is a fact.

In 1995, I read an incredible book called *Creative Visualisation,* by Shakti Gawain. This book is the original manifestation bible. At age eighteen, most of the messages passed me by, but the one that stuck with me was the message that I could choose what mood I was in. It made me realise that I could always choose how I wanted to feel. With that realisation came such power. I felt as though someone had given me a small part of the secret to life itself.

Over the years, I haven't always lived true to that realisation! I have experienced extreme self-doubt, I have had heartbreak, I have had very difficult health issues to deal with and I have lost people I loved. We cannot choose how we feel in these situations, but we can choose how we react to those feelings. We can support ourselves through those feelings and less-than-ideal moments using the tools and exercises we learn about in this book.

USEFUL MANTRA

Something amazing will happen today.

EXERCISE 3.1

SHAKE YOUR BODY

1. Pick one song that absolutely lights you up,
2. Put it on,
3. Dance like no one is watching (even if they are),
4. In the car,
5. In the kitchen,
6. In the shower,
7. Standing on your bed,

8. This is a failsafe way to lift your mood.

We've all heard about kitchen dancing, right? Well guess what, there is method in the madness. A really good shake, wiggle, shimmy or jiggle is guaranteed to make you feel amazing. The science shows that when we connect ourselves to a particular song, the likelihood of it improving our mood is increased by over 60%!

RESIST THE URGE TO HIBERNATE

If you are feeling low in mood or outlook, there is one very important thing to know. You must really, really try to fight the urge to do nothing.

You know those days when you want to curl up under the duvet and stay there? I hate to inform you, but that is often a fast track to feeling worse. Do not worry, you'd be forgiven for thinking that is not the case. We are bombarded with messages to 'go easy on yourself', 'give yourself a break', but it is scientifically proven that the worst thing we can do when we are not feeling great, is nothing. Our brain and body is designed to keep us safe and to retreat inside our cave, but to break the spell, we need three things; fresh air, movement and connection. It is as simple as putting on a pair of shoes, getting outside, walking and visiting or calling a friend.

I need you to exercise some sense and logic in this section. If you are unwell, you do need rest. What I am talking about here are those times when you're just not feeling it - you're not actually poorly but you don't have your usual va-va-voom. These are the times when self-compassion takes the form of a caring, compassionate kick up the arse.

Last year, for many months, I was feeling lost, hopeless, pretty helpless and overwhelmed. There were so many days when I really wanted to pull the duvet back over my head and stay there. There were so many days when I did pull the duvet back over my head and stay there (admittedly, usually after I had done the school run). I was procrastinating during the day time, neglecting work tasks, feeling overwhelmed by home tasks and on some dark days, I didn't want to have to face any of it.

Even though I knew, deep down, that getting on with stuff was going to make me feel good on so many levels, the resistance was huge. We are programmed to keep ourselves safe and have been doing this for centuries. If we have had our feelings hurt, our brains tell us to not use feelings anymore and to go through life without feeling. If we are not engaging with our feelings, they can't be hurt, can they? After heartbreak, we declare we are never falling in love again. After failure, we declare we are never trying again. After loss, we declare we are never becoming attached again.

Thankfully, that doesn't last forever!

I give you permission to feel.

I give you permission to fail.

I give you permission to lose.

In fact, just today, in the middle of writing this, I have seen a video posted by a well-known creator where she criticises the famous motivational coaches (Mel Robbins, Jay Shetty, Lisa Nicholls et al) for suggesting that we push ourselves to do something, even if we are not in the mood. I speak in more detail later in the book about Mel Robbins' book, *The 5 Second Rule*, but having that motivation to get on and do something is vital for ALL of us most of the time. The creator suggests that we should perhaps 'take a nap' instead. I cannot emphasise how unhelpful this approach is. So many people do not need permission to take a nap. They need support to get up and get out and DO STUFF THAT MAKES THEM HAPPY.

If you need a nap that much, you really need to do something concrete to check your energy levels. The occasional nap is obviously totally amazing, totally permitted and totally fabulous. We just have to make sure we are not napping to avoid living life.

As always, I am sending love and joy to that particular creator who was just going for a laugh in the moment. I guess some things just land harder than others.

SPEND TIME WITH YOUR TRIBE

In 2010, when I was pregnant with my first child, I joined a pregnancy yoga class called Yogabirth. It was run by a lovely - and slightly bonkers - woman called Linda. I had a car accident when I was nineteen weeks pregnant and although it wasn't particularly serious, my pelvis became twisted, which meant I struggled to sleep for more than five minutes at a time. This meant I spent most of the yoga birth classes asleep. Thankfully, I still carried on showing up anyway as it was my best nap of the week (see, naps are allowed!).

I had spied a woman I wanted to be friends with at one of the first sessions and made a beeline for her. She was suffering from pregnancy SPD and was struggling to walk. I offered to pick her up for our classes going forward. We clearly made a formidable duo. As our due dates grew closer, we made a coffee date with a couple of other expectant mums. We found our tribe.

I love this example because it supports the theory that we meet those with aligned values when we do the things that we truly love doing. In this case, the linking factor was yoga. For you, it probably won't be yoga; it can be anything at all, but you have to love it.

If you are ever feeling as though you need a mood booster, a quick call or message conversation with someone in your tribe can be the best medicine.

If you don't have a tribe, please do not despair. Skip (or wait to get there) to Chapter 6, where you will learn why and how to create aligned and fulfilling relationships. We all have a tribe out there, no matter how bonkers you think you may be (believe me, most people really do think that they are bonkers). It does take a little effort and putting yourself out there to find them but you really will be so thankful that you did.

Your tribe is your vibe and will always have your back. so go and hang out where they will be and make them yours!

EXERCISE 3.2

POWER POSING

   1. Think of your favourite superheroes, standing strong and fearless in the face of an emergency.

The chances are that you have imagined them in their signature power poses. Wonder Woman with her hands on her hips, Superman with his arms outstretched flying.

2. Find a space where you have plenty of room (if at work, an empty meeting room or even a toilet cubicle will work perfectly!), and stretch out your arms and legs.

3. Now put yourself into your OWN superhero power pose and stand and hold it confidently – no matter how ridiculous you feel. No one can see you!

4. It is scientifically proven that adopting these power poses releases hormones that make us feel more capable and powerful.

5. Use this whenever you feel the need to boost your mood.

CASE STUDY: EMILY

I had known Emily for many years as our children were born around the same time. Emily came to me to find out about joining the Flourish course as she was feeling pretty awful. She hadn't slept well for years and she had very little joy in her life. She adored her four children and they had become everything to her, but in the process of parenting, Emily had completely lost herself. She didn't feel depressed or anxious, but she just had a low-level lack of energy and joy.

In our first session, I asked Emily when she had last done something for herself. After a few seconds, she broke down. She was absolutely mortified because she couldn't think of a single thing that she had specifically done for herself in weeks.

Emily explained that she was waking up tired every day, feeling groggy all day and wanting to go to bed, then going to bed and not sleeping. The never-ending cycle.

The first thing we did was implement the LIFE elements.

1. Fresh air,
2. Movement,
3. Water,
4. Nutrition,
5. Rest.

Emily began taking her daily walk as soon as the children had left for school. She walked for forty-sixty minutes each morning. The benefit of doing your healthy life habits in the morning, is that they are done. Nothing can derail them. You also end up with a fantastic sense of accomplishment, which is a wonderful start to the day.

The final exercise Emily used was setting herself three mini fun tasks each day, no matter how low she was feeling when she woke up. Sometimes this was as simple as watering the plants, other times it might have been setting aside ten minutes to call her elderly aunt.

Emily slowly started to feel more energised. It isn't a quick fix and she experienced many ups and downs along the way, but she began to realise how great she felt after the morning walk - she even woke up looking forward to it. She was joined regularly by a couple of friends and so, the walks became a great opportunity for them to catch up. This led to Emily joining another local chat and walking group, which became a highlight of her week.

Emily began to realise that she was in a much better position to support her teenage children when she was supporting herself.

EXERCISE 3.3

THREE GOOD THINGS

This is probably the most powerful of all positive psychology exercises and one that has been, and can be applied in so many different ways and circumstances.

The instructions are very simple.

Every night before bed, for one week, take the following steps:

1. Think of three things that went well for you during the day.
2. Write them down.
3. Reflect on your role in them.

For this exercise to have the most impact, it is vital to write the three things down, as it helps you really focus on the events. Equally, reflecting on your role in them contributes to the impact on you. In some circumstances, this may not seem relevant, for example, if one of the good things was the glorious weather. In such circumstances, we note down that we noticed and appreciated the good weather and the positive impact this had on the way that we felt.

This exercise has been extensively used and tested all over the world. It has been shown to increase happiness and decrease depressive symptoms.

Every morning, as we wake up, we have the power to choose our mood. We have literally no idea what is going to happen to us that day, but in the moment of waking up, we get to choose how we approach the day.

On the days when you do not wake up in a great mood, there are so many things you can do to help yourself. This book is full of stories, ideas, tools, exercises and techniques that you can use to give yourself a raring start.

None of this should make you feel under pressure. I know what that feels like and it is hideous. There is noise and advice coming from every direction and you feel as though you should be actioning it all, while simultaneously feeling as though you can barely get dressed. In these moments, strip it right back. Get connected to your go-to methods: walk, breathe, talk to someone, focus on the good stuff and love yourself so, so deeply.

As with all of this book, this is not medical advice and if you feel you need to, please contact a medical professional.

There are also great local groups that welcome people of all ages who may struggle with low mood and they are a great place to look for support and understanding.

USEFUL MANTRA

I choose to be bright. I choose to uplift myself when I need to. I choose to honour my feelings while maintaining that my power lies in my response.

4

FOCUS

> *'Where focus goes, energy flows.'*
>
> — TONY ROBBINS

> *'Focus more on your desire than on your doubt, and the dream will take care of itself.'*
>
> — MARK TWAIN

Focus, focus, focus. Focus pocus.

What do we actually mean by focus?

I would simply say a definition would be 'the ability to concentrate on the task at hand without being distracted'.

The world is a very different place from the one we loved ten or twenty years ago. In our hands, we carry around a tiny, yet incredibly powerful machine which instantly gives us access to pretty much everything in the world.

YIKES!

Just take a moment to let that settle in. We can do everything (pretty much) with something that we can fit in our pocket. We have instant answers to our questions. We can order whatever we need. We can listen to any song in the history of music at the touch of a button. We can speak to people no matter where they are in the world. Who had any idea that the handy mobile phone would turn into the world in our pocket?

The number one issue that I am contacted about at the moment (spring 2023), is people wanting help with their lack of focus. It is really, really affecting people's lives. Instagram, TikTok, Snapchat, Discord and a million other platforms that I haven't heard of - are constantly buzzing away in your pocket, begging for your attention. As I have been sitting here writing this morning, my family group on Telegram has been discussing cream cakes! And of course, there is no doubt that these pocket devices have been amazing at enabling us to constantly be in touch with our loved ones, but at what expense?

QUALITY TIME

The reason that people contact me about their perceived lack of focus, is that they don't feel happy about their use of their phones, particularly regarding social media, Youtube and other endless applications. They feel that it negatively cuts into their family time, their relaxation time, their creativity and productivity. So, how do we change that?

How do we stop feeling as though we are letting our devices steal our time?

The first thing to remember is that beating yourself up does not serve any positive purpose. It really doesn't. Instead, be more specific about how you DO want to spend your time. Schedule non-phone time into your day. You can even set usage limits on your devices to help you implement usage goals.

The most important thing though, is to remind yourself of the things you do love doing (create your own list):

- Playing an instrument,
- Meeting up with friends,
- Crafts - knitting, painting, upholstery,
- Working out,
- Gardening,
- Fishing.

Once we reconnect ourselves with these pursuits, we begin to create new neural pathways that enable us to reestablish patterns and habits that do serve our well-being.

WHAT IS A NEURAL PATHWAY AND WHY IS IT RELEVANT TO WELL-BEING?

Neural pathways are the routes that information travels through the brain, allowing us to perform various mental and physical functions. They are essentially the connections between different regions of the brain that enable communication and signal processing.

Neural pathways are made up of networks of neurons, which are specialised cells that transmit information via electrical and chemical signals. When information is received by a neuron, it triggers a chemical reaction that causes an electrical impulse to travel along the neuron. This impulse is then passed on to other neurons.

The connections between neurons are not fixed but can change over time in response to experience and learning. This process, known as neuroplasticity, allows the brain to adapt to new situations and learn new skills. Neural pathways can also be strengthened or weakened through repeated use or disuse, a phenomenon known as synaptic plasticity.

Different types of neural pathways are involved in different functions, such as sensory processing, motor control, memory and emotion. For example, the visual pathway is responsible for processing visual information from the eyes, while the motor pathway controls movement and coordination.

The study of neural pathways is important for understanding how the brain works and how it is affected by various conditions and diseases. Researchers use techniques such as brain imaging and electrophysiology to study neural pathways and their role in different functions. This knowledge can be applied to develop new treatments for neurological and psychiatric disorders, such as stroke, Alzheimer's disease and depression.

THE POWER TO CHANGE YOUR OWN BRAIN

The brilliant and exciting thing about knowing this is that it is literally the power to change our own brain! When I found this out, I was so excited! Just because we have been doing something a certain way for years and years, does not mean that we can't undo that brainwave pattern. Our brain has muscle memory in the same way that our body does, and we can retrain and exercise it in the same way.

I love this piece of knowledge because it feels so empowering. Nothing is beyond our control and we can never use defeatist phrases again because they don't hold any weight! Phrases such as 'That's just the way I am' and 'You can't teach an old dog new tricks' are officially redundant and we can be free of the shackles they impose upon us.

HOW DO I SHUT OUT THE 'NOISE'?

This is one of the questions I am asked the most at the moment. It comes from all kinds of people, but particularly those who are desk-based for work, and even more so for those working from home. We have seen a huge shift towards working from home over the last three years, which may seem wonderful in many ways. As with every-thing though, there can be downsides and it is really healthy to acknowledge that sometimes, working from home is not always as easy as it may seem.

Over the last five years, I have worked: from home, from a co-working space, in my own office, in a shared office, from home and back to a co-working space. I clearly like things varied! I recently did a mini-audit to find out where I had created my best QUALITY work - so, not my most amount of work, but the highest quality work in terms of creative output. I was astonished to find that it was in a co-working space that, at the time, I didn't think I liked at all!

I now have a varied mix between my home office and a co-working space. My current co-working space is in a theatre, which I LOVE because I find it so inspiring to be surrounded by creatives and I absolutely love it when the soundchecks for the shows are taking place. I am a musical theatre nut.

There are certain specific things we can do to support ourselves in an environment that can help us create our best work. What this might look like for each of us could be wildly different. Some of my clients love working in Costa and Starbucks. That is my idea of hell! I am way too nosy and would end up people-watching and eavesdropping and would get precisely nothing done!

I regularly go to a gorgeous health club and every now and again, I have an amazing day working there. That works particularly well if I am doing practical work such as numbers, scheduling and booking systems. It does not work for writing though.

For writing, I have a very specific set of criteria but the best thing is, I KNOW it works! It is like a switch that I can flick and I am in writing mode.

What are my flow conditions?

- Clear space - no mess or clutter,
- Classical music - usually quiet and gentle,
- Oil diffuser - I have a favourite blend from Revive,

- Consistent access to tea and water,
- Having already had a decent walk outdoors.

When I have all these things, I am confident that I have put myself in a good position to be able to write. By the way, there are no guarantees! Some days, I write a tenth of what I may have done the day before and some days, I read back and don't like what I see, but I do know that I have given myself the best chance when I have created my flow environment.

WHAT IS FLOW?

Flow is a positive psychology concept that describes the state we reach when we are at our creative best.

Creating a flow environment typically involves a few steps, depending on the specific context in which you want to create it. Here are some general steps you can follow:

- Identify the purpose of the flow environment: Determine the specific goal or problem that you want to solve using a flow environment. This will help you determine what tools, resources and processes you will need to include in the environment.

- Define the nature of the environment: Determine the boundaries of the flow environment, including what tasks, workflows or systems it will cover. This will help you define the environment.

- Identify the tools and resources needed: Determine what tools and resources you will need to build the flow environment. This may include apps, hardware (such as lights and headphones), data sources (books or research papers) and anything else.

- Create the flow: Build the flow itself, using the tools and resources you have identified.

- Test and refine the flow: Test the flow environment to ensure that it is functioning as intended. Identify any problems or issues that arise and refine the environment to address them.

- Implement the flow: Once the flow environment is complete, implement it whenever and wherever you need.

Overall, creating a flow environment can be a complex process that requires careful planning and attention to detail, however, with the right tools, resources and processes in place, it can help you streamline workflows, automate repetitive tasks and improve productivity and efficiency.

HOW TO GET MORE FLOW INTO YOUR LIFE

There are a number of rules you can follow which will help you get more flow into all domains of your life.

- Set a SMART goal. SMART means:
- *Specific.* Is your goal well-defined? Make sure you know exactly what you want to achieve.
- *Measurable.* Your goal needs to be measurable in order to know when it is achieved.
- *Achievable.* We all have our own version of this. We need to push ourselves while also making sure that we can actually achieve our goal.
- *Realistic.* Can we actually make the goal happen? Is it within our power?
- *Time-bound.* You need to set a target date and allow sufficient time to achieve the goal.
- Aim for a high skill/challenge balance. We need to be challenged enough that the goals stay interesting and exciting, but they must not be so technically difficult that we feel we don't have enough skill to achieve them.
- MINIMISE distractions (see above).
- Set up a method to receive immediate or very quick feedback. This is such a great motivator.
- FUN! Make it fun and enjoy yourself.

WHAT IS MENTAL CLARITY?

Mental clarity is a state of mind where you feel fully present, engaged and active. You are clear of thoughts and mental fog which means you can focus on what you need to do, when you need to do it. Learning how to increase your mental clarity and prevent those negative thoughts is a skill that will enhance all areas of your life.

You know those days when your mind is on *fire?* Where you are coming up with amazing ideas, when you smash your action lists and achieve even more? They feel so good, don't they? Well, guess what? There is a recipe to create days like that. When I found this out, I was over the moon. This means that we can have so much control over the way that we feel. We are not just a boat bobbing around an ocean, being tossed and turned by the waves; we are the captain of this ship and we are taking it to great places!

The recipe varies from person to person and it can take a while to work out exactly what you need, but it is seriously worth the effort.

The main ingredients are:

- sleep,
- water,

- fresh air,
- movement/exercise.

When I want to focus, I make sure that I concentrate on 'hope theory'. Motivation alone is not a long-term plan. As we have seen before, there are a number of environmental factors that can support us when we need to focus. Equally, there are some scientifically-proven frameworks that we can use when we want to focus on longer-term goals and plans.

Hope theory offers a framework for how we set goals, create pathways to achieve goals and how we maintain motivation when we achieve goals. Hope theory argues that if we do not believe that we can achieve our goals, and if we do not identify the pathways to achieving the goals, it is unlikely that we will achieve our desired goals.

> *'Hope happens when your rational self meets your emotional self in the pursuit of clear 'want to' goals that excite you, with multiple pathways to help you navigate the obstacles and commitment to take actions necessary to see them through.'*
>
> — DR MICHELLE MCQUAID

The Hope Map (below) is probably every positive psychology coach's favourite intervention and this is because it is so effective. At first glance, it can sometimes seem a little simplistic, but do not be fooled! It is one of the most powerful and applicable interventions we use and it always gets results.

FOCUS IN WORK AND BUSINESS

When it comes to focus on a work basis, the Hope Map is an incredible tool and one that many of us use several times a week to help us plan and stay on track. Because it enables us to identify obstacles at the outset, we have already identified them and we can follow the plan we have created to overcome the obstacles and make progress. It's like magic.

EXERCISE 4.1

THE HOPE MAP

Step 1: Set Your Goal

Determine a clear and exciting vision of a goal that you would like to achieve.

Step 2: Identify Pathways

Write down several actions, pathways or steps you will take to pursue the goal.

Step 3: Identifying Obstacles

Identify at least one obstacle that might block each of the paths you have described.

Step 4: Identify Pathways to Overcome Identified Obstacles

Moving back to the Pathways section, review your existing pathways, including strategies to overcome the obstacle identified. This may include developing new pathways altogether or building additional steps to your existing pathways.

Step 5: What is your goal 'Why'?

Write down why this goal is meaningful to you and how it is aligned with your values. What will happen, or how will you feel if you do not achieve this goal?

Step 6: Identify your Support System

Do you need support to help you achieve your goal? Write down your support system.

We can use the hope map for anything that we want to achieve. It is a really simple, effective system to work out what you want to do and what steps need to be taken to make it happen. Remember, to make a change you have to GET STUFF DONE. The sooner you start, the sooner the changes are going to happen. So, come on, start now! What is stopping you?

CASE STUDY

Ellie came to see me because she wanted a career change but 'knew' that it wasn't possible. She had three young children and her husband's work as a self-employed silversmith meant that his income varied considerably from month to month. Ellie had been in her career as a senior physiotherapist for twenty years, ever since she qualified. She found her career stressful, draining and restrictive and she spent many hours in the evenings doing paperwork. Although, deep down, she still loved helping people to recover, her passion for the profession had gradually been eroded by the changing demands of the job and she really didn't enjoy it at all anymore.

Her passion was her art, which was creating fused glass artworks. She had enjoyed this as a hobby since she was a teenager and she was really trying to get back to doing it regularly in her spare time because she knew how much it helped her feel joyful and happy when she was able to create.

OFTEN, THE ANSWER IS IN PLAIN SIGHT

Ellie completed the hope map exercise and had a huge realisation - she wanted to turn her hobby into a business and become the creative that she had always wanted to be. By going through the steps of the hope map, she realised that she had been creating obstacles around why this would not work, but by identifying the pathways to overcome the obstacles, she suddenly realised that it was entirely possible to overcome. The obstacles she thought were preventing her from embarking upon her artistic career were, in fact, not obstacles once she was able to identify what she could do to overcome them.

Ellie was able to connect with her goal of being a full-time artist and realised that her 'why' for doing this was completely aligned with all of her values which were: creativity, freedom, beauty and wholeheartedness.

HOW TO APPLY THIS TOOL TO YOUR LIFE?

You can use the hope map exercise as often as you need to. It can be applied to a huge variety of situations and once you become familiar with using it, it can be very easy to run through the steps of the hope map naturally. We almost do it as second nature in many situations, which ultimately makes us super solution-focused.

PROCRASTINATION

We use this word a lot more in recent years than we ever have before, but what does it actually mean? It is generally accepted to describe the times when we have something that we need/want to do, but rather than get on and do that thing, we find other things to do instead, meaning the original thing doesn't get done.

There are many reasons why we procrastinate but the main one is fear. Often, if we don't know how to do something, we will put off starting because we don't know how. If you do this, believe me, you are in good company. Pretty much everyone does this to a certain extent. What we need to do is create ways of getting out of it as soon as we realise we are in it.

CIRCUIT BREAKERS

You need to come up with your own set of circuit breakers. Circuit breakers are tasks or activities that you know will help you snap out of the procrastinating mood.

As always, my first option is to go for a walk. You have the combination then of fresh air, movement and adrenalin – all of these things act as a circuit breaker when we are procrastinating. When you get back home, all rosy-cheeked, you can crack straight on with the task you need or want to get done.

THE SCROLL OF DOOM

As I mentioned above, this is a pretty new one for us all to navigate. Between beautiful house renovations on Instagram, to weight loss stories on Tik Tok, to beautiful cakes on Pinterest – never mind, reels, YouTube shorts, Facebook watch and a million other options that I don't even know about, the internet (aka, the world in your pocket), is a very time-consuming place to be. It literally STEALS time from you. Not only that, the companies who make these videos know exactly what to do and how to draw you in, so they are intending to keep that dopamine hit going FOREVER.

I am guilty of doom-scrolling, particularly if I am tired or feeling under the weather, or if there is something really big and important that I have to do but I don't know where to start.

I am afraid there is only one thing for it here – DISCIPLINE. We need to make social media work FOR us and not let it use us.

- Set yourself app time limits, like you probably do with your children.

- Set a specific time each day to use social media, i.e., thirty minutes, twice a day and no more.
- Be honest with yourself when you don't want to do something and create a flow environment that will help you do it (for me, this is an abundance of tea, Classic FM, fluffy socks and my oil diffuser).

SIMPLE REMINDER

- What are the obstacles?
- What pathways can I use to overcome them?
- What is my 'why'?
- Who else do I need to make this happen?

EXERCISE 4.2

TAKE THE WIN

If you have a goal that you are trying to realise but negativity or procrastination is getting in the way of making it feel possible, try this visualisation exercise.

In an upright seated or lying down position, straighten the length of your spine. Close your eyes and picture a medal on a ribbon. Feel the satisfying weight as the medal is placed over your head and around your neck. Imagine the colour of the ribbon, the thickness of the material attached to the metal resting on your chest.

Take the cool metal in your hand and feel the weight. Notice that the medal has some text written on it. Read what the text says. Remember how reading those words made you feel.

This is a wonderful exercise to do with children too, when they want to channel a winning attitude, perhaps before a sporting competition or an exam. It is a great tool to be familiar with because it can simply and quickly change your whole mindset about whatever challenge you are about to face.

The most important aspect to remember is not to beat yourself up when you find yourself procrastinating. We could all do that forever and it won't get us anywhere. Instead, acknowledge that it is happening and decide what you will do to snap yourself out of it.

Focus on how brilliant you feel when you have accomplished a specific task and, invariably, how much easier it was in reality than you thought it was going to be.

Find which circuit breaker tool works for you best and make that a new habit as soon as you feel you need it.

USEFUL MANTRA

I know how to stay focused when I want to. I have the tools and exercises I need to help me concentrate.

5

COURAGE

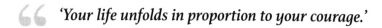 *'Your life unfolds in proportion to your courage.'*

— DANIELLE LAPORTE

WHAT IS COURAGE?

When I think of courage, I think of the Cowardly Lion from the Wizard of Oz.

Courage is an indispensable skill. Life requires courage, yet, like the Cowardly Lion, many of us are only afraid of our own tail. What we are afraid of can feel like life itself, when in actual fact, we are afraid of a whole raft of things - failure, heartbreak, pain, death, disappointment, illness, loss... the list goes on.

We tend to lose sight of its meaning, and instead, we consider the courageous ones to be the obvious: daredevils, paramedics, frontline heroes and those who risk themselves to help others. What we really need to focus on singularly, is the courage to be truly ourselves. Free of the fear of judgement of others.

HAVE THE COURAGE
Donna Ashworth

Have the courage
To live as a whole.
To listen to your heart,
To talk to your soul.
To know who you are,
When others do not,
To look out for your vibes,
To filter your thoughts.

Have the patience,
To wait for the signs.
But never stop living,
Enjoying the ride.
Listen for the silence,
As loud as the screams.
Respect life's sorrows,
Follow your dreams.

These wonderful words from Donna Ashworth capture perfectly for us, what it means to have courage. That is, to follow your dreams.

It takes a whole heap of courage to follow your dreams. It takes courage to even share what your dreams are.

COURAGE TO BE YOU

A few years ago, I was on an amazing Sound Goddess course, where we learnt to use sound therapy for healing. During one meditation, I had a vision of a mythical god opening a curtain to reveal I was on a stage, speaking to thousands of people. It seemed crazy at the time and I felt embarrassed to share it. Who was I to be speaking on a stage to thousands of people?

When I shared my vision, I was met with great whoops and excitement from everyone in the room with me. It was an amazing feeling because if they thought it was possible - maybe even a message - then maybe I could believe it, too. The feeling made my heart swell. Do you know that feeling? When your heart literally feels as though it is swelling? That is where the word courage comes from. The French word for heart, *coeur*, forms the basis of courage. Your courage is in your heart.

Courage is not the absence of fear, but moving ahead despite fear. Courage is the empowering experience of a decision to stand up and withstand whatever criticism, rejection or mockery might come your way:

To embrace reality, rather than retreat from it,

To tolerate, rather than cower or ignore,

To persevere, rather than quit.

The VIA Institute is dedicated to bringing the science of character strengths to the world. The VIA Institute describes courage as 'the exercise of will to accomplish goals in the face of adversity or opposition, whether internal or external'.

We must remember that although we are born with an instinctive sense of fear, it is only there to keep us alive. It doesn't prevent us from speaking to certain people, or from saying how we feel in certain situations. Did you know that the only fears human beings are born with are the fear of falling and the fear of loud noises. This makes perfect sense.

Throughout our lives, our experiences, the people around us, the way we are treated and a whole host of other factors begin to impact and chip away at our courage. We fall over in the playground, someone laughs and our fear of judgement kicks in... and we lose a little bit of that natural courage.

HUMAN VS ANIMALS

You may often hear humans being compared with animals to either validate or question some of our behaviours. The thing is, we are not animals. We are homo sapiens and have evolved away from the instinctive drives that keep animals alive. Our fears come from role-modelling. We learn from our parents, who learnt from their parents. My friend is scared of birds and so are her children. My grandad didn't like to travel abroad, my mum isn't wildly keen either. These are not coincidences. One situation literally produced the next. No one is to blame here and in actual fact, it makes it easier for us to unravel. Once we identify the source of a fear, it becomes much much easier to face it head-on, get underneath it and work out how to triumph against it.

I often have people tell me that I am brave, either because I have been speaking on a stage to hundreds of people, or I have bought another property, or I have spoken up for someone who wanted representation, or I have been inter-viewed on the TV or radio. I find this interesting because, to me, it was something that needed doing, whether for work or another reason. To be able to do that kind of thing,

I have a strategy - I plan, I follow it through and I execute it. When I do feel scared (and I always do), I know that breathing will make a huge difference. I have made it a priority to understand breath work and how it can be used to calm the central nervous system. To me, there is a problem and a solution. As long as I know how to apply the solution, I can solve the problem.

I have always been very literal and have interpreted things in a transparent way. Sometimes, it gets me into trouble! But it also allows for a very simplistic view of life which definitely can resolve some of the nuances that often derail us.

EXERCISE 5.1

I CAN HANDLE THIS

Step 1: Take a pen and paper and write down a really difficult thing that you have been through.

Step 2: Close your eyes and for five minutes, take yourself back to that time and feel the feelings that you had during that time.

Step 3: After five minutes, take the pen and paper again and write as much as you can about how you overcame those things, about what you did to be able to cope with them. Write down how significant they are to your life now.

Step 4: Write yourself a letter explaining how grateful you are for the way you have dealt with the incredibly difficult things in life and be really specific about the reasons. Tell yourself how brilliant you are. Put the letter in an envelope and put it in a book that you read regularly or in a drawer, so that you may come across it in the future.

CASE STUDY

Gemma was a client who came to me when plagued by back problems which were massively affecting her life and work. The impact was also affecting her mental health and her GP had suggested Prozac. Gemma was not keen to start medication because she believed that the low mood and depression were being caused by the pain in her back and that the problem with her back would not be fixed by anti-depressants.

Gemma continued to work with her chiropractor and we had weekly sessions to understand the impact it was having on her well-being. Gemma came to realise that there were two main reasons she was feeling so low. She'd had to give up her work as a community nurse and she had been unable to attend her weekly netball practice. She felt that she had lost her sense of purpose and belonging, and she was starting to doubt who she was. This meant that she had started to feel fear about work and socialising, and that had been preventing her from doing the exercises to help her back.

Gemma used the 'I can handle this' exercise (see Exercise 5.1) above every morning, evening and whenever else she needed it. She found the confidence to start moving her body more and, with the support of her chiropractor, was able to return to work with a slightly adapted role.

When I caught up with Gemma recently, she was a different person. She bounced towards me, with a grin as wide as her face. 'It was all in my head', she said. Well, it clearly wasn't, but there were significant mental blocks there preventing her from healing. It was a delight to see Gemma looking like a different person and radiating warmth and joy.

POSITIVE PEOPLE ARE LUCKY PEOPLE

Being lucky is simply a matter of perception. It is said that people make their own luck. This is simply another way of saying that they perceive their life differently. Many people suffer the absolute worst adversity and still consider themselves lucky.

I have worked with people this year who have suffered from the most hideous experiences;

- Rape,
- Cancer,
- Murder,
- Bankruptcy,
- The tragic death of a partner,
- Release from jail,
- Addiction and crime,
- Incurable disease,
- Burns victims.

The list can go on but I am sure you can see what I am trying to show you. These people have experienced the absolute worst things that we can ever imagine happening to human beings, yet they are still grateful for life.

It is so wildly inspiring to know that there are people who have been through experiences way worse than we will ever have to experience, who are still embracing life and finding the positives in every day.

I would never want to diminish your own experiences but simply, I want you to realise that you can do this too. You can have the perception of life which means you can reframe and decide what your approach to the next day is going to be. Every single day.

PUBLIC SPEAKING

One of the most widely-reported fears for adults in the UK is public speaking. Whether this is a presentation at work, or speaking to a group of people we know, it continues to be something that so many people find incredibly difficult. It is made all the more difficult by the fact that so much of our emotion can be held in our throats, which means when we are anxious, we can lose our voice.

There are a number of breathing techniques that can help considerably with this. The Alexander technique is used widely by presenters, singers and performers. There is much data and evidence now to show how much difference it can make when we take control of our breathing patterns.

When we focus on the fear, we are giving weight and substance to that fear. When we focus on the outcome, we take that weight away and we can focus on what message we want to leave people with.

It can be very effective to have actual tools to rely on in these situations. You may have come across some herbal potions and remedies that help give us courage. Bach Rescue Remedy is one that many of us are familiar with. It is a blend of flower remedies. It is designed to help people deal with immediate problems and many people choose to carry it in their handbag, in their car or keep it on their desk at work. I use an oil blend called Courage, produced by an essential oil company called Revive. My children love to roll it on their wrists when they have performances, exams, interviews or assessments.

It doesn't really matter how much the actual ointment helps in these circumstances. It is more about having a routine you can rely on that you know will help ground and calm you. The sense of courage itself comes from the routine and knowing that you have validated your own fear, and have done something material to help.

EXERCISE 5.2

STAND FIRM LIKE A TREE

A great way to ground yourself when you are in the midst of fear or turmoil is to connect with the earth. We came from the earth and we go back to the earth. When we have lost connectivity with our courage, we need to re-establish our roots with the earth beneath our feet.

Stand firmly on both feet and take some deep breaths. Visualise roots growing from your feet into the ground.

Stand firm, like a tree, while the chaos around you blows through your branches and disappears on the breeze.

This is a wonderful grounding exercise and it will significantly help increase your courage and self-assuredness. It is particularly effective if you can do it bare-footed on the grass. We are given a direct connection to the earth via the soles of our feet which makes us feel so much more solid and secure.

PREPARATION

If you really are worried about performing or doing a specific presentation, it is true that preparation is the best way to gain courage. I am not much of a planner - I am happy to wing most situations now, particularly when it comes to public speaking, however, that is largely because I know my topic so well. I live, breathe and teach positive psychology and it exudes from me most of the time! I often joke that if I was cut in half, I would have positive psychology written through me like a stick of rock!

Preparation and practice will give you so much courage. Try not to leave things until the last minute. Instead, give yourself time and space to work out what you need to know and do to feel prepared. This applies to everything we need courage for, from sports events to giving birth. The more you know you have prepared, the more you will feel able to take on your challenge with fortitude and gusto.

It is also great to record yourself multiple times in advance, most laptops have this function. You will be able to see which areas are tripping you up and also, you will be able to adapt your delivery as you can see yourself doing it.

BE BRAVE

I want you to do something, now that you have all of this new knowledge, that is really brave. Choose something that you really want to do but that you have not had the courage to do before. It may take a while to think what this could be. Is it to apply for a new job that you don't think you would get in your wildest dreams? If you don't apply, you will never know. Is it to ask someone on a date? Is it to go for a big promotion? Is it to quit your job and start a business? Is it to tell a family member how they made you feel?

Whatever it is for you, give yourself some time to mull it over because most adults, particularly men, are really, really bad at admitting that they need courage. When I speak with such clients, they are adamant that they are not afraid of anything and that they don't let fear get in their way. It takes ages to unpack then, why they aren't in a certain position at work, or why their business has not grown in the way that they had planned or expected.

Muscle memory applies to courage and bravery too. The more we exercise our courage, the more comfortable we get with using it and the more likely we are to use it again and again in the future.

IT'S NOT FEAR, IT'S EXCITEMENT

Courage is a funny one. Many of the people I work with do not see themselves as lacking courage. They are not where they want to be in life, but they do not attribute their situation to a lack of courage or self-belief. Instead, they are far more likely to look around themselves and blame it on other external factors.

It takes a lot of courage to admit that you are lacking in courage. It is much easier to blame our circumstances on things outside our control, such as the government, the weather, the economy and a whole host of other reasons.

When we take responsibility and are vulnerable enough to admit that we do not have courage, we are only then in a position to start creating it. By using the exercises and examples outlined in this chapter, you will begin to build a toolkit that you know works for you and that you are comfortable with. It can be applied in any situation and you will have the strength within to work through fear and into courage.

We only have to do things a few times before they become much easier. That is the beautiful thing about courage, the more we exercise it, the stronger it becomes. Muscle memory applies to our brains too. The more we can show ourselves that we can achieve something, the more we believe it. When you can say to yourself, 'I have done this ten times before, I can do it this time', you are much more likely to believe that to be true.

USEFUL MANTRA

I can handle this. It's not fear, it's excitement.

6

RELATIONSHIPS

> *'Friendship that insists upon agreement on all matters is not worth the name. Friendship, to be real, must ever sustain the weight of honest differences, however sharp they be.'*
>
> — MAHATMA GANDHI

W e have all heard the saying that we are the sum of the people that we spend the most time with.

We cannot underestimate the impact that our close relationships have on our well-being. Just one conversation, with one person, can change the whole trajectory and approach to our day, so it is incredibly valuable to have tools and methods to deal with the impact of those around us.

I want you to know right now, that it is absolutely OK to have less-than-perfect relationships. We can't fix everything, and nor should we try.

When I am working with clients, relationships are often one of the most difficult topics to broach. From a well-being perspective, when we talk about relationships, we mean all relationships with all the people in our lives. This includes:

- Partners,
- Parents,
- Siblings,
- Family members,
- Children,
- Neighbours,
- Colleagues,
- Friends.

Basically, anyone that we interact with on a regular basis.

This is because they all form an important part of our lives, particularly if we see or speak to them regularly.

It is a tough topic because so many people have difficult relationships and they cannot see how to change that. The good news is, there are really effective ways of improving those relationships and also limiting the impact of any negativity on ourselves when we do experience it.

FAMILY

Plenty of us have complicated and difficult relationships with our families. Some of us even have no contact with various family members and we don't have great memories or perceptions of our family.

The one thing to remain clear on here is that we cannot change other people - not directly, at least. Nor do we ever need to try. It is actually not our business to try and change other people, they can only do that for themselves.

Many people find it really tricky to navigate this area because they don't feel that they have uplifting, positive relationships with their close family. They feel that some family members are actually the most difficult relationships they have. These difficult family relationships can make it very difficult to see them in any positive light at all.

One of the most useful explanations of this comes from the incredible Louise Hay, in her book, *You Can Heal Your Life*.

'If your mother did not know how to love herself, or your father did not know how to love himself, then it would be impossible for them to teach you to love yourself. They were doing the best they could with what they had been taught as children.'

— LOUISE HAY

'They were doing the best they could with what they had been taught.' Many of us find such solace in this approach and it enables us to move through towards forgiveness.

ROLE-MODELLING

The most effective way of changing the dynamic of any relationship is via role-modelling. Instead of being drawn into toxic situations, destructive disagreements and petty arguments, we can choose not to be drawn in and instead, stay authentic to our true selves. This shows others around us that a) we are not in the mood to tango, and b) how they can also choose to not engage in the toxic stuff. It may or may not work, but it does mean that you protect yourself from being drawn into the toxicity. It really does take two to tango and the power of being able to walk away from what you know will not serve you is incredible. What happens when you don't engage is that you become the circuit breaker. This is a really empowering position to be in because you are not feeding the situation and, after a while, the toxic element to it may begin to subside.

EXERCISE 6.1

THE FORGIVENESS LETTER

Step 1: Think of a person from your past whom you are holding resentment towards or have been in conflict with.

How is holding on to this affecting you? How is it affecting the other person?

Studies of forgiveness have shown that forgiving does not mean forgetting, condoning, pardoning or excusing the transgression – and, importantly, the goal of forgiveness is not always reconciliation.

Rather, forgiveness is something you do for yourself in order to reduce your level of psychological distress through the release of toxic negative emotions. It has been said that the opposite of love is not hate, it is indifference. Hating someone takes just as much energy as loving them, with the direction of the energy being the only difference. The negative energy and emotion that you put into not forgiving can, over time, contribute to major negative health outcomes, while the person who committed the transgression against you suffers no further ill effects due to forgiveness.

It seems that by not forgiving, you allow the situation to victimise you all over again and for an indefinite amount of time. Essentially, forgiveness allows you to take your power back. That being said, forgiveness is something that you must freely choose to do and is something that may take some hard work.

Step 2: Write a letter of forgiveness

To help you get started down the path of forgiveness, you write a letter in which you describe a situation or event that made you sad or uncomfortable and the emotions related to that situation.

Then pledge to forgive the transgressor, but do not send or discuss the content of the letter with the person you write it to.

The purpose of this exercise is to help you experience the power of forgiveness, even in the absence of feedback. Hence, your letter can be written to someone you are no longer in contact with or someone who may already have passed away.

Write your forgiveness letter on a separate sheet of paper – there is no right or wrong here, just let it flow.

Step 3: When you have finished writing your forgiveness letter, answer the following questions.

1. What did it feel like to write your forgiveness letter?
2. Do you feel ready and willing to commit to forgiveness? If not, why not?
3. How did you feel to read your forgiveness letter?

BOUNDARIES

Relationships are the area of our lives where boundaries are tested the most. This can be in our romantic relationships, at work, with our children or with our friends. One of the best quotes I read about this is,

 'Having boundaries doesn't make me a bitch.'

This was a genuine revelation for me. I really thought it did mean that! I thought turning people down, saying no and exercising my own free will was bad manners! Hello, people-pleaser! Thankfully, those days are becoming less and less frequent the more I get to identify how I think I should behave versus how I want to behave.

SCARY WOMEN

When I started university, I considered myself to be fairly strong-willed and independent. I had spent a year travelling the world, I was open-minded and principled and was a pretty good debater. I definitely had the words, and the balls, to argue my point of view in any given situation, or so I thought. It turns out, I was actually way better at arguing on behalf of other people than I was for myself! In fact, it had never occurred to me to stick my head above the parapet on my own behalf. The very idea of it made me squirm. I was well and truly happy, putting up with my lot, no matter what it was or how uncomfortable/dissatisfying or inappropriate that may have been.

I had two friends in particular (when they read this, I am pretty sure they will know who they are!), who basically just made a nuisance of themselves all the time. Well, at least that is how I saw it. They demanded more for themselves, they spoke out whenever they felt they deserved more, they spoke loudly and consistently and were absolutely sticking their heads above the parapet. They asked for more respect, they demanded more pay and they were comfortable making requests for extra skills to enable them to progress professionally - I was in awe! I thought I found them really annoying. Well, in my head they had become annoying. Now though, I realise that I was fully triggered because I knew they were standing up for themselves in a way that I never had.

ASSERTIVE

I'm not sure if I even knew what the word assertive meant at this point. The whole concept was quite alien to me. I had been taught (and role-modelled) to do as I was told, not make a nuisance of myself, respect authority and generally comply. So, even with all my head-strong, go-getta-girl attitude and having travelled extensively around the world by the age of nineteen, I was still completely restricted by the societal expectations I had been taught to comply with. Actually, it was worse than compliance, it was not even to question.

I actually perceived these women as a nuisance! I saw them as belligerent, annoying and generally a pain in the backside. Not a single part of me could see that they were standing in their truth. I was so indoctrinated at that point to be a 'good girl'.

For centuries, women have been told to stay quiet, keep small and obey. Women were persecuted for leaning into their own magic, for connecting to nature and for following and leading through intuition. We are mothers, nurturers and powerful beings of nature. We have to push past millennia of oppression and conditioning to rise into our true place and stand up for ourselves and for future generations.

How this manifests itself in our relationships plays a significant part in how they evolve. A true, equal, mutually-beneficial relationship is one where all parties are free to express their feelings without fear or judgement or persecution.

We need to ensure that we are in a relationship where we do have the freedom to express ourselves effectively.

If this makes you realise that you may need to talk to someone, First Light provide a confidential helpline for all genders (https://www.firstlight.org.uk).

INTRODUCING MORE POSITIVE ENERGISERS INTO OUR LIVES

Scientifically speaking, it is actually possible to catch a vibe from - or pass a vibe onto - someone else through positive energy. That is, when a person in your close contact has a positive vibe, research shows you are likely to feel more positive emotions, too, and if that person is a colleague or manager, you could even be more productive and successful at work. But the energy-passing can also work in the other direction, with negative relational energy having an overall de-energising effect on everyone involved. So, it's worth your while to consider both where the relational-energy peaks and valleys lie around you, and how you might be contributing to either, in order to maximise the positive energy you ultimately feel.

In this way, the more time we spend with people who are positive energisers, the more positive vibes we absorb from them. How great is that? We can actually take on the positive energy emitted by those around us. However, this means that we can also absorb negative energy from those around us too. What is actually more likely to happen is that certain people drain us of our uplifting and positive vibes. You may have heard them referred to as energy drains or energy vampires.

I am not wildly keen on either of those descriptions because they almost suggest that the energy drains are doing it on purpose. I don't believe that to be the case. They subconsciously emit their own energy, which has the ability to bring us down if we are unaware.

Positive energisers are active and exuberant, responding to challenges with a desire for action. Most of us will be able to easily identify who in our lives are the positive energisers and who are the energy drains.

MY POSITIVE ENERGISERS

One of the most significant positive energisers I have ever had was my friend, who is just about to turn eighty-five. My friends are all wonderful and I love them dearly, but they don't always occupy the role of positive energiser. This particular lady and I hit it off the moment I met her. I have always had a habit of having much (much) older friends, particularly women. I love the sense of worldliness and wisdom that they exude. I always feel I absorb some of that wisdom just by listening to the stories of other people's lives and experiences.

I met this particular lady in 2015 when I had just moved to Cornwall with my family. It was a time of huge change and transition. I spent much of it working out where and how we all slotted into our new lives, over 400 miles away from the London street we had moved from.

As we had bought a forest, I needed to up my horticultural game quickly! I was barely able to tell a beech tree from an ash back then and I was trying to work out how to deal with a plantation of Japanese Knotweed bigger than most people's gardens! I had tree surgeons, arboriculturalists, gardeners, groundworkers and all sorts to be dealing with. I had never done any gardening, nor had I had any interest in it, but here I was, with ten acres and a forest so, I was in head first. My friend and I started gardening together. We mainly pulled brambles because the whole place was so completely overgrown. We spent hours and weeks together, chatting, sometimes silent, sometimes learning, often laughing while getting to grips with the brambles and weeds.

What I now realise is that the whole experience became my grounding moment. It was where I laid my roots in Cornwall. It was where I found my place, and where I refined it. What I learnt from that friendship has no words. The fact that I can now identify a hellebore is a cute, but inconsequential part of that relationship.

Be open to welcoming new positive energisers into your life. They are everywhere and they have so much to offer, and you to them. We do have to be open and accepting of new and varied people for them to be able to take that role.

I used to hold a salon gathering for interesting people that I knew. It is something I have always done, not really knowing why. It was borne out of the realisation that I knew so many wonderful, positive and amazing people, but that they didn't know each other. So, I was drawn to connect these amazing strangers to each other. At one of these salons, I had women ranging from fifteen to eighty-five years old. So, be open-minded about what your positive energisers might look like, you might be surprised.

HANG OUT WITH PEOPLE WHO MAKE YOU FEEL AMAZING

The good news is, as ever, there are plenty of steps you can take to take active control of the relationships in your life. The first step is to identify who makes you feel amazing, and the second is to spend more time with them. Simples!

1. Identify the people in your life who make you feel amazing.
2. Spend more time with them.

This leaves two main issues to be addressed. One: what if you don't feel as though you have enough, or even any, positive energisers in your life? Two: how do you find more?

WHAT WE PUT OUT, WE ATTRACT BACK

This is where we circle back to mood booster. Science shows that we are far more likely to make long-lasting aligned connections when we are doing a hobby or an activity that we enjoy. That is because, people with similar values are attracted to similar recreational hobbies, pastimes or volunteering.

Have a think: how many times have you known someone to meet their partner at the gym, or in a sports club, or at a charity event, or a music group? The same happens with friendships, business partners and new acquaintances - we are far more likely to connect with them when we are doing something that aligns with who we are. This provides us with even more reason to create new habits, where we do something purely for pleasure at least once or twice a week.

ARE YOU THE KIND OF PERSON YOU WOULD WANT TO HANG OUT WITH?

If you met you at work, in a meeting or at a sports club, would you want to hang out with you? If yes, hooray! If not, why not? The natural magnetism within the universe means that like attracts like. If you are looking to meet someone far more energetic, lively, ambitious, driven or vibrant than you, the likelihood is that it won't happen. What you need to think about first is how YOU can become those things yourself and then you will begin to magnetise more people like that into your life and your world. Even setting the intention to do that will make a huge difference to the energy that you are putting out there which will, in turn, begin to attract more energetic people back to you.

THE GOLDEN SPHERE OF PROTECTIVE ENERGY

The most wonderful thing about the relationship element is that it is scientifically proven that the more time we spend with our positive energisers, the less impact the negative energy drains have on our lives. We are so topped up with feel-good emotions and chemicals from our interactions with those that lift us up, we become almost immune to the impact of anyone who previously had the capacity to bring us down.

I like to describe the golden glow as a cloak, a force field. The more time we spend topping it up, the stronger and more impenetrable it becomes. I want you to picture a beautiful golden orb that lowers itself over your whole body. It floats around with you wherever you go. When any arrows of negativity are thrown your way, they just bounce off, powerlessly. They cannot penetrate the beautiful spinning protective energy of your golden orb.

This is by far the best way to approach dealing with family members who you may have previously had a difficult relationship with. Whenever you spend time with them, you can flick the imaginary 'on' switch on your golden orb and watch the insults or moaning ping to the floor as they bounce off. Earlier on, we discussed how this often starts to unravel the energy drain and, without any interaction, the dynamic of the whole relationship may change and improve over time.

CASE STUDY

Della is a women's empowerment coach and she specialises in trauma-informed therapy. A former social worker, she moved into coaching after she had experienced a personal transformation following a marriage breakdown after years of emotional abuse and controlling behaviour. Della was healing well and her business was thriving, which was doing wonders for her well-being via her sense of connection with meaning and accomplishment. Della was stuck on her relationship with her parents. She was carrying a continual resentment and knew that she was stuck in a pattern of behaviour that she had been in since childhood. Della's parents had expressed their disappointment that Della's marriage had 'failed', in spite of the fact that she had taken pains to explain the extent of the emotional abuse. They also believed that she had thrown away her successful and important career in favour of launching her own coaching business. Della felt judged and reverted into child mode whenever she spent time with her parents, which left her feeling drained, worthless and unloved.

Della had grown up in a household where codependency had evolved between her parents. Although not explicitly abusive like Della's own relationship, she could recognise the patterns of behaviour that had led to her deprioritising her own well-being in her own marriage. Della wanted to rebuild her love of her parents while protecting herself from any shame they felt about her and free from being affected by judgement or criticism.

Della's favourite pastime was netball and she hadn't played regularly for many years. She joined a local group that practised weekly and immediately clicked with the other women in the team. She also reconnected with some of her university friends who she had not seen much over the past ten years or so, and they began planning meet-ups a couple of times a year.

Over a number of weeks, Della agreed to do a visualisation each day, where she saw a protective golden bubble grow stronger and stronger around her. She agreed set times to visit and spend time with her parents and she made sure that her protective bubble was firmly in place during their meetings.

I am delighted that Della was able to find a great dynamic in her relationship with her parents and that they will be able to enjoy a strong and beneficial relationship over the years.

THE UNCOMFORTABLE TRUTH

I have to mention this part here, because the chapter on relationships would be incomplete without acknowledging this. It is absolutely fine, and necessary, to end relationships either temporarily or permanently if that is what you decide you need to do. There is no rule that we have to keep people in our lives if they are truly affecting our well-being, even if it is our parents, siblings or partner.

When we grow on a personal level, those around us don't always grow with us. In fact, they rarely do. They may see changes in us that make them uncomfortable. We become more assertive, more demanding and more articulate about what we do and don't want.

There are so many incredible professionals now who are equipped to help and advise in these situations and I would urge you to make contact if you feel as though you are in this situation. You may be pleasantly surprised that there is a way forward when you didn't think there was. You may be seeking permission or validation to make the big decisions, and that is perfectly understandable.

When seeking professional advice, please do always check that the practitioner has the relevant qualifications and insurance.

EXERCISE 6.2

ACTIVE CONSTRUCTIVE RESPONDING

Researchers have identified that there are four main styles of responding to good news in a relationship. The one we consider to be the most supportive and nourishing is known as active constructive (AC) responding. This works for all kinds of relationships, including romantic, professional, friends and family.

When we are AC listening, we give the person we are talking to our full attention. We give them full, unbridled and enthusiastic support for whatever they are telling us and we allow them to savour the moment of telling us the good news. This may involve saying things such as, 'wow, that's amazing, please tell me all about it' or 'That's such brilliant news, you must feel great'. To respond in this way, we need to be fully connected to what the other person is telling us and it has even more impact if we repeat choice phrases and words to underline the meaning of what they have said.

It can take some practice to be able to do this naturally and authentically, but it is a wonderful skill to develop and so therefore, one worth taking the time to master. When you can respond in this manner, you are helping make the other person feel even better about the good news they are sharing and clearly showing your support for them.

You may be able to think of people you know that do this already. I remember the first few times I encountered AC responding (I obviously didn't know it had a name back then), and it made me slightly uncomfortable. It was such an enthusiastic and supportive response style, I had not been used to it before and it made me question whether the person's intentions were real. That definitely says a lot more about me than it does about them and it is something I now actively practise all of the time. It leaves me feeling so much more connected with everyone around me and I find that I retain facts and details so much better.

One of my favourite books is the classic, 'How to Win Friends and Influence People', by Dale Carnegie. It is both wonderful and incredibly simplistic at the same time. There is just one message from that book, and the message is LISTEN. If you accompany the listening with nodding and eye contact, you are onto an absolute winner, but just listening really is the key.

So many of us spend much of the conversations we are involved in, waiting for our turn to speak. We sometimes barely register what anyone else is saying because we become so focused on what we are going to say. This might mean we miss out on huge chunks of the conversation, but it also means we are disengaged and can appear so to everyone else. This impacts forming deep and trusting relationships because everyone wants to feel heard by those they care about.

My work has taught me that listening is incredibly important in forming quality relationships. As a coach, we need to spend all of our time listening. If we didn't, we wouldn't be able to work with the client effectively. One of the easiest ways to make sure that we are actively listening is to gently repeat what the other person is saying in our head as they are talking. This means that we take the words to a deeper subconscious level and are so much more engaged and connected with the conversations.

VISUALISATION

I want you to picture yourself in a small, cute cafe. There is a gathering of people and one is about to stand up and talk. As they start talking, you realise that you are repeating every word they say along with them in your head. You feel so connected to the words, the person speaking and the message that they are delivering. When the person stops talking, you feel as though you can almost remember what they said, word for word.

If you would like to practice active listening, you can listen to the radio and try speaking along, repeating the words of the presenter. You can even use the cafe scene as part of your visualisation as this will make it easier to connect to and digest the words being said.

It is an incredible, but also a fun skill so have great fun mastering it. It will always be useful.

Let's take this opportunity to celebrate all of the amazing relationships we have in our lives. People really are our EVERYTHING!

We are not the direct result of our relationships. We can take ownership and responsibility for the impact our relationships have on our well-being and we can invite energising and uplifting relationships.

We have complete autonomy over who we have relationships with and don't ever think that you don't. We are the boss of ourselves and we can choose exactly who to interact with and when. If a relationship is not making us happy and is not energising us, we have a responsibility to ourselves to work out why and what we want to do next.

Positive energisers really are the key to an incredible life. They provide the framework for connection, fun, intellectual stimulus and excitement. We can continue to collect new positive energisers as we go through life. They will come from all different arenas and will adopt completely different roles, but they are all contributing to the general golden glow of energy.

USEFUL MANTRA

I choose to invite and welcome energising, uplifting and positive relationships into my life.

7

FUN

> 'We need Joy as we need air. We need Love as we need water. We need each other as we need the earth we share.'
>
> — MAYA ANGELOU

I thought I would leave the best 'til last. If there is one thing, my darling, that will improve your well-being, it is fun. Silly fun, crazy fun, funny fun, planned fun, unexpected fun and downright ridiculous fun.

If there is one thing that quickly slips away when our well-being isn't doing so great, it is the fun in our lives. We can lose the ability to laugh, to smile even. We don't feel like doing the things that make us laugh and we slowly retreat into a rather serious and sombre existence. 'I'm far too grown-up and busy to have fun', you might hear yourself think. 'I've got far too much serious and stressful stuff on my plate to think about gallivanting or doing anything remotely joyful', is something else I hear regularly.

Do either of these sound familiar? I think they probably do. Fun can be perceived as flippant and unnecessary at times of stress and we actually shut ourselves off from it as part of our stress response. In actual fact, the thing we need the most in those moments is more fun! We need more laughter, more lightheartedness and definitely more joy. I don't know who coined the phrase 'laughter is the best medicine' but they were not wrong!

TOO STRESSED TO HAVE FUN

I often start my sessions with 'What are you celebrating today?' and 'What have you done for fun this week?'. Both of these questions seem fairly simple but they can render a regular adult completely speechless. It is never my intention to make my clients uncomfortable and to see people squirm is awful, but what I then see is the dawning realisation that this is not ok. Most are embarrassed that they can't remember the last time they had fun. They know that they should be having more fun. They know that it is good for them, so to realise that they so rarely have fun that they can't even remember when they last did, comes as a bit of a shock.

Fun is an essential part of life that allows us to let go of stress and connect with our emotions in positive ways. While it might seem trivial, having fun is really good for you psychologically.

Having fun releases endorphins, which are the hormones that make us feel good. These hormones can help to reduce stress, improve our mood and increase our overall sense of well-being. Endorphins are the body's natural painkillers and can also help to boost our immune system.

Fun activities help to improve our relationships with others. Participating in fun activities with family and friends can strengthen bonds and improve our communication skills. It can also help to build trust and create positive memories that we can look back on in the future.

Doing fun stuff also helps to improve our self-esteem. When we engage in activities that we enjoy, we feel more confident and capable. This can translate into other areas of our lives, such as work and relationships, where we may feel more self-assured and capable of achieving our goals.

Taking part in fun activities also helps to improve our cognitive function. When we engage in activities that challenge our minds, such as playing games or puzzles, we improve our cognitive function and memory. This can be especially beneficial for older adults, as it can help to stave off cognitive decline and keep the brain healthy.

A really important point to note here is that having fun can help to reduce the symptoms of depression and anxiety. Engaging in activities that bring us joy and happiness can help to distract us from negative thoughts and emotions. It can also help to boost our mood and provide us with a sense of purpose and meaning.

Having fun is not just a luxury, it is essential for our mental health and well-being. By participating in activities that bring us joy, we can improve our relationships, boost our self-esteem, enhance our cognitive function and reduce symptoms of depression and anxiety.

HAVING FUN IS AN EXPERIENCE OF LIBERATING ENGAGEMENT

What does fun look like for adults? When we imagine children having fun, the images spring to mind easily. We think of playgrounds, theme parks, swimming pools, fun on the beach or playing in the garden. The fun is carefree and fully in the moment. It is enjoying the activity purely for the sake of fun. We can easily conjure up a mental image of what it looks like for children to experience joy and have fun. It is quite different for adults.

WHAT DO I DO FOR FUN

Before I started my studies of positive psychology, my doses of fun were few and far between. In the main, they generally would have revolved around the children - joining them for a day at a theme park, a bike ride, a trip to the beach or a board game. Those things were, and still are great fun. But none of them was fully about me. Our children need to see us as autonomous beings with agency to execute our own fun exactly in the way that we want it.

Now, I make sure that I do something fun every day. Sometimes, it is just about me, sometimes it's about other people, and let's be honest, sometimes it's about the dog! He definitely needs fun too for his own well-being.

- Walking,
- Singing,
- Sea swimming,
- Reading,
- Audiobooks,
- Yoga,
- Radio comedy,
- Chatting with my sisters,
- Dancing,
- Roller skating,
- Tennis,

- Travel,
- Quiz nights,
- Murder mystery,
- Folk music.

There are loads more things besides but this list is a good example of the things I can rely on to have fun.

EXERCISE 7.1

WHEN DID YOU LAST HAVE FUN?

Step 1: Take a pen and paper, and write down all the times you have had fun in the last twelve months*.

Step 2: Choose your favourite of these and write down WHY it was fun. What particular aspects of it did you enjoy?

Step 3: Write down a date when you will next do the same activity.

*If you cannot think of any occasions you had fun in the last twelve months, don't panic, just extend the time frame to two years, five years etc.

As adults, we can have fun in loads of ways, depending on our interests and preferences. The exciting thing is that we totally get to choose! As children, we probably had hobbies and pastimes suggested to us that were based on the preferences of our parents. For example, there is no coincidence when you know a whole family who runs, or sails, because the generational pattern of behaviour is strong here too. As we become independent, we are more aligned with who we are and what we like doing, which leads us to find new hobbies that come entirely from our own desires.

1. Pursue a hobby: Whether it's painting, playing an instrument or gardening, pursuing a hobby can be a great way for adults to have fun and relax.

2. Participate in sports or fitness activities: Joining a sports team, taking a fitness class or going for a run can be a great way for adults to have fun and stay active.

3. Spend time with friends and family: Going out to dinner, watching a movie or playing board games with friends and family can be a fun way to socialise and bond.

4. Attend concerts, festivals or other cultural events: Going to a music festival, art exhibit or theatre performance can be a fun way for adults to explore their interests and experience new things.

5. Travel and explore new places: Taking a trip to a new city or country can be a fun and exciting way for adults to learn about different cultures and try new things.

6. Volunteer and give back to the community: Volunteering for a cause that you are passionate about can be a fulfilling and rewarding way for adults to have fun while making a difference in the world.

7. Engage in creative activities: Writing, drawing, cooking or DIY projects can be a fun and creative way for adults to express themselves and explore their creativity.

The key to having fun as an adult is to find activities that you enjoy and that make you feel good. It is vital to make time for fun activities and to prioritise self-care and relaxation. Often, I recommend that people put the fun into their diaries to make sure that it has the same importance as work and social engagements.

SCUBA DIVING

When I was thirty, I was walking near London Bridge on my way home from work. I glanced up and saw a scuba diving shop and before I knew what was happening, I had walked in and was skulking around, looking at wetsuits and flippers (as I thought they were called then!). As I tried to sidestep my way out of the shop, wondering what the hell I was doing there, a chap approached. I am sure you can guess what happened next. Before I knew what was going on, I had signed up for a 'try dive' the very next day! The shop was also a dive training company and the pool they used was a few minutes walk from my office. There had been a cancellation on the try dive and the spot was mine.

As soon as I arrived home, I was full of self-doubt. Why the hell had I done that? Could I even afford it? Don't people die scuba diving? What was I trying to prove? I spent the whole next day telling myself the same things and trying so, so hard to talk myself out of it. Clearly, there was a determined part of me that wanted to go and a few hours later, I experienced scuba diving, in a swimming pool near Old Street, for the very first time. And I was hooked.

Over the following few years, I spent nearly all of my free time diving. I travelled to Indonesia, Egypt and the Maldives, and I also dived all around the UK. I made some incredible friends because we had this shared aligned love of diving. I became very involved in ecology and marine conservation, connected to my passion for the ocean and marine life, and met even more people who had aligned values and priorities. I even shifted my professional focus to sustainability and environmental standardisation because I could see how vital it was to have aligned thinking on an international level to be able to sufficiently protect marine life all across the world.

FULL CIRCLE MOMENT

We often refer to this as a full circle moment. Why is that? It explains a situation where our passions and interests drive us to become more and more educated in a particular topic and we end up becoming an expert in that topic. Our passion has taken control and has almost created a situation to facilitate becoming our work and the way we make our living.

Have you ever heard the phrase 'love what you do, and it doesn't feel like work?' That describes this scenario. It is possible for so, so many of us if we just listen to what our subconscious mind is telling us. If I hadn't walked into that scuba diving shop that evening, I would never have pursued my studies in the environment and sustainability.

How does this fit into this chapter about fun? It is totally relevant because the more we work out what we find fun, the more joy we invite into our lives and the more in alignment we become. Fun is about so much more than just having a good time, it is an insight into who we really are and what we enjoy doing.

HOW DO WE FIT FUN INTO OUR BUSY LIVES?

In positive psychology, fun comes under the pillar of positive emotions. We learn that we need to feel positive emotions on a regular basis to support our well-being. Although many of us struggle to think when we last had fun, once we explore what fun is for us, we begin to see how and when fun does show up in our lives. As adults, fun doesn't often take the form of running around a playground with friends, but it may well involve running around a football pitch with teammates. Fun doesn't often involve making sandcastles on the beach on our own, but it may do with our children or grandchildren.

Below is a list of some of the ways that I hear about from my clients regularly:

- Playing team sports,
- Playing musical instruments in a band/orchestra/group,
- Golf, tennis, squash,
- Singing in a choir,
- Going to the theatre,
- Knitting, crafting, model-making,
- Faith-based gatherings,
- Meeting up with friends,
- Volunteering.

CASE STUDY: DANNY

Danny and I had been working together because he had been feeling as though something was missing from his life. He was in his late twenties and had started a tech business five years earlier. Business was great, he had a large international team and he was really happy with work, however, he felt as though he didn't know how to have fun. He was incredibly healthy, was a committed runner and went to CrossFit most days, and though all of those things made him feel good, they didn't represent fun to Danny.

Danny and I completed an intervention together called 'What's My Story?'. This involves breaking your life down into chunks (in this instance, decades), recalling pivotal moments from each decade and identifying themes. In this exercise, the experience that stood out the most for Danny was when he competed in a number of international sailing expeditions as part of a crew. He had such amazing memories of the experience, the teamwork, the sense of camaraderie, the fact that others relied on him and he was able to identify that the experiences had been a lot of fun.

Fun can look completely different from one person to the next. We can only connect to what brings us fun and joy when we are being honest with ourselves. We need to let go of others' opinions of us or fear of judgement.

For Danny, it became very clear that he associated his success with being serious and focussed and that to achieve that, he had to let go of anything that he perceived as a treat or frivolous. By doing this, he had let go of the things that energised him, specifically sailing. This also impacted the quality of his connections because they were now mainly work-related. Back on the boats, his sailing crew had become his friends as well as his teammates and he was missing that camaraderie and connection.

Danny, being Danny, joined a local sailing club, bought a new boat, and signed up to a huge charity sailing challenge. We are not all Danny and we don't have to make huge great changes overnight, but his story shows us how easy it is to lose sight of the things that make you, you. We can be too busy to have fun. We can be too stressed to have fun. We can be too blinkered to have fun. We set our sights so firmly on what we think will bring joy and happiness and when it doesn't, we don't know what to do next because we have lost connection with what that looks like for us.

Sailing was for Danny. Singing is for me. You need to find what your fun looks like. You need to make sure it is not someone else's version of fun, but yours and authentically yours. This may take a while to work out but it is truly worth the effort. Some of my clients have discovered a newfound love of drumming, golf, wild swimming, radio presenting, bookbinding, cycling... the list goes on and on.

Make a pledge to yourself to keep trying new things when the opportunity arises. Not only is it really good for us but also may turn into something that becomes an important part of your well-being.

SING LIKE YOU MEAN IT

Singing in a choir is not only a fun and enjoyable activity, but it also has a number of benefits for your physical and mental health. Singing boosts mood, reduces stress and releases endorphins, which are hormones that make us feel good. It can also help to reduce stress and anxiety and improve our overall mood.

- Singing enhances breathing and posture. It requires good breathing techniques and posture, which can help to strengthen our lungs and improve our posture.
- Singing improves cognitive function: Singing requires us to memorise lyrics and melodies, which can help to improve our cognitive function and memory.
- Singing increases social connection: Singing in a choir provides an opportunity to connect with others who share a common interest, which can help to improve our social connection and sense of belonging.

- Singing improves vocal technique: Singing in a choir can help to improve our vocal technique, such as breathing, tone and pitch, which can be beneficial for public speaking or other vocal activities.
- Singing provides a sense of accomplishment: Performing in a choir can provide a sense of accomplishment and pride, which can boost self-esteem and confidence.
- Singing provides a sense of purpose: Singing in a choir can provide a sense of purpose and meaning, which can be especially beneficial for older adults who may be looking for new ways to engage in meaningful activities.

For me, singing in a choir is a fun and rewarding activity that I know makes me feel amazing. Each week, when I get home, I am absolutely buzzing and it definitely makes me feel more alive than an evening at the laptop or on the sofa! I have made friends through my various choirs that I would never have met otherwise.

I am an OK singer. I am not brilliant, I am not awful. I have absolutely no desire to sing solos but I know I am a good solid contributor in a choir. This aspect of having fun is not about being perfect or brilliant. It is not about being the absolute best you can be. It is simply about enjoying yourself.

Go on, go and have some fun. You have my permission!

101 WAYS TO CHILL OUT

Take a pen and paper and write down a list of things that you think might bring you fun. You don't even have to have done any of them before.

A few weeks ago, my sister and I went to a roller disco. We had been to one once before, probably about fifteen years previously, in London, and had a great time zooming around to 80s pop. We arrived at the venue, which is a full-time roller rink, and the car park was empty. We both looked at each other and I could see that flash of self-doubt cross her mind as well as mine. 'What are we doing here?', 'Why did we come? We are too old for this!', the inner voices screamed. As we were given our skates, we both wondered whether we should have turned around in the car park.

Less than ten minutes later, we were both in hysterics, laughing uncontrollably about how brilliant and liberating it was. We were having child-like fun. We felt unburdened of our usual responsibilities of parenting, housework, work, washing and everything else that comes with everyday life. It was such a wonderful evening, we didn't want to stop skating, even though our legs were aching. We vowed to go back.

THE CHILD WITHIN

Our inner child really does need to come out to play on a regular basis. It is a part of us that is vital to our personality and sense of self. We have to be vulnerable enough to let it out and see what it wants to do. The reason that we have to be vulnerable is that we have a fear of being judged for being childish. That inner child remembers being laughed at or having someone tell them that their ideas were silly. That forms such a strong part of our memory, that we feel as though we have to protect that child from any more criticism.

Once we are able to let go of the fear of criticism or judgement, we are free to let the child emerge. Imagine those times when you have had a snowball fight and you are completely lost in the moment of energy and fun. How good do you feel afterwards?

Fun is a vital component of a satisfying, fulfilling and enriching life. We become energised when we have fun. It actually produces more energy to do other things with. It provides punctuation in our weekly schedule where we know we will be experiencing positive emotions. When we have fun, we are more open and accepting and are more likely to meet other people who have fun doing the same things we do. We certainly don't have to love exactly the same things as our partner or friends, but some shared interests go a long way to providing the fabric for fulfilling long-term relationships.

USEFUL MANTRA

I deserve to have fun. I love letting go and enjoying myself without thinking about what anyone else thinks of me.

THE FINAL WORD

Let me tell you about a day, not so very long ago when things felt very different. I didn't want to get out of bed. I snuggled a bit longer. When I did get out, I was cross with myself for wasting time so now the morning would be rushed. I stood in front of the bathroom mirror and did not like what I saw. Puffy eyes, double chin, sticky-up hair - I started saying all sorts of nasty things to myself. 'Look at the state of you, woman', 'Who do you think you are?', 'You look like cr*p!'.

A few hours later, I stood on a stage in front of over six hundred people and spoke for an hour. I shared my lows, my highs, my tips, tricks and techniques I had learnt along the way. At the end, there was a queue of more than twenty people waiting to talk to ME! They wanted to talk to me and say thank you for inspiring them, for making them think, and for being vulnerable and honest with them. I had to smile... in the space of a few hours, I had gone from insulting myself in the mirror, to feeling on top of the world and basking in the glory of having inspired and motivated others.

Why am I telling you this now? Haven't I just given you all the answers? Well, as always, it isn't that simple. Yes and no.

I want you to know that the destination is not fixed. This journey we are all on, called LIFE - it throws in challenges, obstacles and all sorts of other things along the way. There is no 'finished product' when it comes to personal growth and self-awareness. Instead, we are always evolving and that means there will always be ups and downs.

What often happens when we do have those down moments, is that we let them completely derail us. We want to throw the towel in and all of the 'who do I think I am' thoughts come flooding back.

No one has it all sussed.

I remember the first time I saw a graphic saying that we could be two things at once, I suddenly felt totally relieved. You can be smiling and struggling, vulnerable and powerful, successful and traumatised, capable and lost. Just because you are one part of it, doesn't mean you can't be the other too.

You will hear many self-development gurus talking about healing being continual, and it is. That doesn't mean it is a bad thing, it just means we need to get used to learning more about ourselves as time goes on. We evolve too. We change due to our circumstances and the things we experience in life.

SELF-AWARENESS

The conclusion to the conclusion has to be about self-awareness. The moment we begin to be honest with ourselves about who we are is the moment we are able to be our real selves. Let's face it, if we aren't even being true to ourselves, how can we ever be real with anyone else?

So many people go through life claiming that they are 'just trying to be nice', but when I manage to connect with them in a way that enables them to be honest with themselves, they realise and acknowledge that they have judgement and superiority, they are holding on to unhealthy patterns of learned behaviour from their childhood and carrying them through adulthood.

The brilliant thing is, as soon as we know that there is no blame for this and we can heal our way to letting go, the huge great swathes of personal growth are right in THAT moment.

TOXIC POSITIVITY

I couldn't write a book about positivity without referencing toxic positivity. It is an interesting topic and one that could warrant a whole new book.

Positivity, being positive, seeing the positives in life and having a positive outlook are all amazing life techniques. There is nothing dangerous or destructive in them. We all know that we can find silver linings, that we can reframe a difficult situation and that we can provide support to those who need it without invalidating their feelings.

What I talk about in this book is not toxic positivity. Positive psychology is not toxic positivity.

I have included a couple of examples below to explain the difference.

1. Being negative won't help you. Replace with: It's important to let it out. Is there anything I can do to help?
2. Good vibes only. Replace with: I love you through all of your emotional states.

3. You'll get over it. Replace with: You are resilient
and your strength will get you through.

I have used so many examples throughout this book of validation, listening, empathising and being there for each
other. Negative thoughts must never be avoided. There will
always be sadness and grief in our lives. No one should ever
feel that they can't have difficult emotions – we absolutely
need them in order to deal with things. What we have
learned here, and what positive psychology provides, are
the tools to reach for when we are ready.

In that sound bath in 2017, when I was in absolute despair, I
couldn't write the words down fast enough about what an
awful person I was. I was scared and broken and lost and
sorry. I didn't know it then, but that was a most beautiful
moment for me, as it was the true start of my journey.

When you have come out the other side, there is such a
huge part of you that is so, so grateful, you just want to
share it with as many people as possible, how they can do
that too. And that's what this is.

Thank you, thank you, thank you.

This book is intended to provide helpful information on the subjects discussed. It is not meant to be used to diagnose or treat any specific medical condition. Please be certain to consult with your own medical practitioner before making any decisions that affect your health.

This book contains the author's interpretation of positive psychology, and the author's adapted versions of the interventions and exercises.

Names and identifying details of some of the people portrayed in this book have been changed.

ABOUT THE AUTHOR

Faye Edwardes is an entrepreneur, property developer, author, writer, podcast host, positive psychology coach (PPCMC) and ever so proud leader of the Positive Living Movement, helping people across the world transform their lives and business by integrating positivity into their lives in a healthy and sustainable way.

An entrepreneurial mum of two, who has run a number of businesses, Faye has overcome self-doubt and overwhelm to thrive in business, property and as a motivational speaker. Faye, a former sustainability professional, is now on a mission to empower people, no matter what their background or circumstances, to take action and take control of their own happiness and well-being to FLOURISH in whatever they choose to do.

FAYE'S STORY

Having grown up in the North West of England, Faye was always an outgoing performer. From the age of five, Faye adored being on the stage, studying ballet, modern, tap and stage at the local dancing school. The annual performances were the highlight of her year.

By the age of 9, Faye had had a number of roles in various dancing shows and performances. Being academically blessed, Faye enjoyed school, found it fun and easy, and was surrounded by friends. By the time senior school came around, teenage self-doubt started to rear its head with a vengeance. Faye became her own worst critic, suffered from weight issues and low self-esteem, began to hide behind her academic work and stepped down from the limelight. At this point, Faye became worried about what other people thought and was surrounded by people who criticised those who put themselves out there. She was taught to manage (i.e., minimise!) expectations and was advised to keep her feet on the ground. Her hopes of a broadcasting career, intentions of working in far-flung places and ideas of earning super money started to seem unlikely.

Over the following few years, Faye enjoyed academic success, spent an amazing gap year in Madagascar and Israel and completed a degree at Queen Mary University of London. By the time Faye entered the world of work, she wasn't the confident, shiny bright thing she had been as a child. Though happy enough, she always had the niggling feeling that there was more... there was something more out there and at some point in the future, she would be in the position to find out what it was.

Faye spent the next ten years enjoying a successful career in sustainability and publishing. In this career, Faye, who is just as passionate about sustainability now, was instrumental in international standardisation and initiatives such as environmental reporting, carbon footprinting, water footprinting and carbon neutrality.

WE BOUGHT A FOREST

In 2015, Faye and her family made the huge move from South London to a forest in the middle of nowhere in Cornwall. It was a huge, exciting challenge that provided the platform for the start of the personal growth journey that was to change the direction of the rest of Faye's life.

In 2016, Faye had the epiphany that started the most exciting and important journey of her life so far. Faye had been to a sound bath with some friends and had a really difficult experience. The sound journey had pushed her to acknowledge the uncomfortable, painful parts of her mind and her soul and Faye felt as though she had failed at everything. All she could focus on were the parts of her life that were not where she hoped they would be.

Faye started to reach out to other successful business-women and began researching tools that would help improve the way she was feeling. Over the next couple of years, without realising it, Faye developed a tool kit of skills, knowledge and techniques that she could rely on when she needed them. Faye qualified as a sound therapist, meditation leader, reiki practitioner and NLP practitioner. She began meditating regularly, cut out alcohol and adopted an early morning routine, and very quickly, her outlook and mindset started to shift.

PODCAST SUCCESS

Faye started her first podcast in 2018, *The Confidence, Happiness and Positivity podcast,* which received an award nomination. Inspired by her alcohol-free lifestyle, Faye launched the *Sober Stories* podcast in 2019. Both podcasts are available on all major podcasting platforms.

In 2023, Faye launched the hilarious *101 Ways to Chill Out* podcast, which casts a raised eyebrow over the whole wellness industry, with many laughs along the way.

POSITIVE PSYCHOLOGY

Having read, *Now is Your Chance*, by Niyc Pidgeon in 2017, Faye had been actively applying the principles of Positive Psychology to support her well-being without really understanding the underlying science.

In 2019, Faye began studying Positive Psychology and in 2021 became a certified Positive Psychology Coach with the PPCA (Positive Psychology Coaching Academy) under the amazing guidance of Niyc Pidgeon and Melanie Deague. Faye was immediately drawn to positive psychology because of the fact that it is a science and all of the interventions and exercises are scientifically proven to be effective.

Faye continues to study positive psychology and is now a Master Positive Psychology Coach with the PPCA and is also a consultant coach for a number of other international organisations.

Faye now works with people all over the world and, using her own golden glowing energy, helps people to change their lives and business dramatically. In 2019, Faye founded the Positive Living Movement and the Positive Mindset Academy.

THE POSITIVE LIVING MOVEMENT

The Positive Living Movement is a free community for people all over the world, who want to make small, achievable changes to their daily lives to significantly increase their happiness. Every single one of us can play a huge part in improving our own well-being, our own mental health and our own happiness.

THE POSITIVE MINDSET ACADEMY

The PMA creates practical courses for hundreds of different industries, so professionals can incorporate a positive mindset in their day-to-day lives, jobs and projects.

Faye's impact:

Faye has been recognised as an outstanding motivational speaker for a wide variety of audiences, including property, corporate, entrepreneurs, schools, charities and entertainment.

Faye is also passionate about sharing her message with the future generations of leaders, parents, business owners, corporates, educational organisations and training institutions.

For interviews, case study information, speaking engagements or comment opportunities, please contact:

Faye Edwardes

hello@fayeedwardes.co.uk

For all book bonuses, worksheets and related information, please visit www.fayeedwardes.co.uk/book

Website: www.fayeedwardes.co.uk

Join my free Facebook community:

www.facebook.com/groups/positivelivingmovement

Social Media

facebook.com/fayeedwardes

instagram.com/faye_positiveliving

FURTHER READING AND REFERENCES

Here's a list of some of the books and websites mentioned which you might enjoy:

Boniwell, Ilona. (2012). *Positive Psychology in a Nutshell.* Open University Press.

Cam, Adam. (2021) *Savage Wisdom.* Adam Cam.

Edwardes, Faye. (2021) *The Science of Happiness: From the Ashes; She is Ignited.* Authors & Co.

Gernville-Cleave, Bridget. (2018). *Achieve Lasting Happiness: A practical guide to positive psychology.* Icon Books.

Goggins, David. (2018). *Can't Hurt Me.* Lioncrest.

Hadfield, Sue. (2012). *Brilliant Positive Thinking.* Pearson.

Hay, Louise. (1984) *You Can Heal Your Life*. Hay House.

Hollis, Rachel. (2018). *Girl Wash your Face*. Thomson Nelson.

Igloo. (2019). *How to be Positive and Happy*. Igloo Books.

Jeffers, Susan.(1987). *Feel the Fear and Do It Anyway*. Ballantine Books.

Lindenfield, Gael. (1989). *Super Confidence: The woman's guide to getting what you want out of life*. Thorsons.

Nestor, James. (2021) *Breath: The New Science of a Lost Art*. Penguin Life.

Nicholls, Lisa. (2010). *No Matter What*. Hachette.

Notaras, K. (2018). *The Book You Were Born to Write*. Hay House.

Pidgeon, Niyc. (2017). *Now is Your Chance*. Hay House.

Robbins, Mel. (2021) *The High Five Habit*. Hay House.

Robbins, Mel. (2017). *The 5 Second Rule*. Post Hill Press.

Seal, Moorea. (2016). *52 Lists to Happiness*. Sasquatch Books.

Wallace, Dani. (2020). *I am the Queen Bee*. Authors & Co.

Printed in Great Britain
by Amazon

33510974R00110